MODERN NOVELISTS

General Editor: Norman Page

MODERN NOVELISTS

Published titles

E. M. FORSTER   Norman Page
WILLIAM GOLDING   James Gindin
MARCEL PROUST   Philip Thody
SIX WOMEN NOVELISTS   Merryn Williams
JOHN UPDIKE   Judie Newman
H. G. WELLS   Michael Draper

Forthcoming titles

ALBERT CAMUS   Philip Thody
JOSEPH CONRAD   Owen Knowles
FYODOR DOSTOEVSKI   Peter Conradi
WILLIAM FAULKNER   David Dowling
F. SCOTT FITZGERALD   John S. Whitley
GUSTAVE FLAUBERT   David Roe
JOHN FOWLES   Simon Gatrell
GRAHAM GREENE   Neil McEwan
HENRY JAMES   Alan Bellringer
JAMES JOYCE   Richard Brown
D. H. LAWRENCE   G. M. Hyde
DORIS LESSING   Ruth Whittaker
MALCOLM LOWRY   Tony Bareham
GEORGE ORWELL   Valerie Meyers
BARBARA PYM   Michael Cotsell
MURIEL SPARK   Norman Page
GERTRUDE STEIN   Shirley Neuman
EVELYN WAUGH   Jacqueline McDonnell
VIRGINIA WOOLF   Edward Bishop

MODERN NOVELISTS
SIX WOMEN NOVELISTS

Merryn Williams

Olive Schreiner
Edith Wharton
F. M. Mayor
Katherine Mansfield
Dorothy L. Sayers
Antonia White

St. Martin's Press
New York

First published in the United States of America in 1988

Printed in Hong Kong

Library of Congress Cataloging-in-Publication Data
Williams, Merryn.
Six women novelists.
(Modern novelists)
Bibliography: p.
Includes index.
Contents: Olive Schreiner—Edith Wharton—
F.M. Mayor—[etc.]
1. English fiction—Women authors—History and
criticism.   2. English fiction—20th century—History
and criticism.   3. Women and literature.   I. Title.
II. Series.
PR116.W55   1988   823'.009'9287   88–6435
ISBN 0–312–02089–9

Contents

Acknowledgments

The author and publishers wish to thank the following who have kindly given permission for the use of copyright material:

Virago Press for extracts from *The Hound and the Falcon, Beyond the Glass* and *Frost in May* by Antonia White;
Gollancz and Dorothy L. Sayers for extracts from the works of Dorothy L. Sayers;
Constable Publishers for extracts from the works of Edith Wharton.

Every effort has been made to trace all the copyright holders but if any have been inadvertently overlooked the publishers will be pleased to make the necessary arrangement at the first opportunity.

General Editor's Preface

The death of the novel has often been announced, and part of the secret of its obstinate vitality must be its capacity for growth, adaptation, self-renewal and even self-transformation: like some vigorous organism in a speeded-up Darwinian ecosystem, it adapts itself quickly to a changing world. War and revolution, economic crisis and social change, radically new ideologies such as Marxism and Freudianism, have made this century unprecedented in human history in the speed and extent of change, but the novel has shown an extraordinary capacity to find new forms and techniques and to accommodate new ideas and conceptions of human nature and human experience, and even to take up new positions on the nature of fiction itself.

In the generations immediately preceding and following 1914, the novel underwent a radical redefinition of its nature and possibilities. The present series of monographs is devoted to the novelists who created the modern novel and to those who, in their turn, either continued and extended, or reacted against and rejected, the traditions established during that period of intense exploration and experiment. It includes a number of those who lived and wrote in the nineteenth century but whose innovative contribution to the art of fiction makes it impossible to ignore them in any account of the origins of the modern novel; it also includes the so-called 'modernists' and those who in the mid- and late twentieth century have emerged as outstanding practitioners of this genre. The scope is, inevitably, international; not only, in the migratory and exile-haunted world of our century, do writers refuse to heed national frontiers – 'English' literature lays claim to Conrad the Pole, Henry James the American, and Joyce the Irishman – but geniuses such as Flaubert, Dostoevski and Kafka have had an influence on the fiction of many nations.

Each volume in the series is intended to provide an introduction to the fiction of the writer concerned, both for those approaching him or her for the first time and for those who are already familiar with some parts of the achievement in question and now wish to place it in the context of the total *oeuvre*. Although essential information relating to the writer's life and times is given, usually in an opening chapter, the approach is primarily critical and the emphasis is not upon 'background' or generalisations but upon close examination of important texts. Where an author is notably prolific, major texts have been selected for detailed attention but an attempt has also been made to convey, more summarily, a sense of the nature and quality of the author's work as a whole. Those who want to read further will find suggestions in the select bibliography included in each volume. Many novelists are, of course, not only novelists but also poets, essayists, biographers, dramatists, travel writers and so forth; many have practised shorter forms of fiction; and many have written letters or kept diaries that constitute a significant part of their literary output. A brief study cannot hope to deal with all these in detail, but where the shorter fiction and the non-fictional writings, public and private, have an important relationship to the novels, some space has been devoted to them.

NORMAN PAGE

Introduction

In the memorable year 1900, Olive Schreiner was interned in war-torn South Africa writing *Woman and Labour*; Edith Wharton was living in the United States with her husband and had just brought out her first short novel; Flora Mayor had published no novels yet, but was living unhappily with her parents in England and hoping to become an actress. Kathleen Beauchamp was a schoolgirl in New Zealand; Dorothy Sayers a child growing up in the Fens; Eirene Botting a small infant in London.

They were all born in the second half of the nineteenth century, but in four different continents and with forty-four years between the oldest and youngest, and so far as I know, none of them ever met any of the others. All were old enough to experience the First World War, though at second hand; none, as it happened, had a husband or son at the front. By 1914 they were all in Europe (the three who were born outside it having fought very hard to get there). Olive Schreiner, her best-known novel thirty years behind her, was in England, sick and out of the mainstream but still protesting against the war. Edith Wharton, now a famous novelist, was helping to organise the French war effort. Flora Mayor and Katherine Mansfield were living on the fringes of the war and doing what they could to put it out of their minds. The two youngest were still students when the war broke out and inherited a world which, everyone agreed, had been transformed.

But there had been enormous and far-reaching changes long before that – in most spheres of life, and especially in the position of women. I was asked to write this book as a kind of sequel to my *Women in the English Novel 1800–1900* (1984), which tried to describe what was happening to English women in the nineteenth century and how the novel reflected this. The

changes continued into the twentieth century, and they are
certainly not yet over. Women got the vote in New Zealand
when Katherine Mansfield was a child, and in England just
after the war. The other great change in their situation was
that, in the 1890s and afterwards, middle-class girls began to
leave home. They got jobs or did war work; they were affected
by the sexual revolution, the loosening of family ties and the
weakening of religious belief. Whereas nearly all the Victorian
novels I studied finished with the heroine getting married, this
is not often the case in the novels of these six women – or in
many serious twentieth-century novelists, come to that. Their
heroines die, go mad, are tried for their lives, or end up
emotionally alone.

Why these six and not others? I was forced to exclude some
distinguished women writers, such as Virginia Woolf, because
they already have books to themselves in this series. I chose
these particular novelists (Katherine Mansfield is not a novelist,
strictly speaking, but both the general editor and I felt that she
should not be excluded) because I admired them and felt that
in some cases – such as Olive Schreiner's *From Man to Man* and
both Flora Mayor's novels – their work had not had enough
attention. All the books I discuss are easy to obtain, many
having been reprinted in the last few years as Virago Modern
Classics. I have tried to give an adequate account of each
woman's personal literary achievement. But there is a connecting
theme, and that is the experience of women in societies which
are undergoing massive changes and giving them confused and
contradictory messages. The central character is almost always
a woman who cannot fit in.

I was not looking for connections between their private lives,
but I found them. They were all striking and unconventional
personalities, who cared a good deal about issues outside
themselves. Half of them came from a clerical background and
religion was an important question for at least four. Five out of
six suffered from a very severe physical or mental illness which
profoundly affected their work. They were all either childless or
had little contact with their children, and all had great problems
in their closest relationships. I am not suggesting that this need
always be so, but it is part of the price that unusual and
pioneering women have traditionally had to pay.

I am grateful to Lyndall Passerini for reading the chapter on
Antonia White.

MERRYN WILLIAMS
May 1986

Note on Citations

In this text, quotations from the author's works are identified by chapter and part where applicable. A single number in parentheses following a quotation indicates the chapter where the passage appears; two numbers indicate both the part and the chapter. Thus, (3) means Chapter 3 and (2,1) means Part 2, Chapter 1.

1

Olive Schreiner

Olive Schreiner is remembered as the first and probably the greatest South African novelist. She grew up in a 'colonial culture almost bare of serious books',[1] and as her compatriot, Dan Jacobson, has written, 'a colonial culture is one which has no memory'.[2] Like Katherine Mansfield, born thirty years later, she got much of her material from a people and a landscape that had never yet appeared in literature. She has had a deep and lasting influence on younger South African writers. Her influence on other women, as novelist and thinker, has been just as important.

She was the daughter of a missionary couple who had come out from Europe to civilise and convert the natives. The Cape Colony where she grew up was considered a British outpost (the Union of South Africa dates only from 1910). Her father, Gottlob Schreiner (the original of Otto in the *African Farm*), was German; her mother, Rebecca Lyndall, had an English nonconformist background. Olive, the ninth child, was born at the remote mission station of Wittebergen on 24 March 1855. She had no formal education and her childhood was fairly unhappy; her mother, she said later, was a brilliant woman but without maternal feelings. One of Rebecca Schreiner's surviving letters complains of 'living as we do among gross sensual heathen,'[3] and she also despised the Boers; in future years Olive was to champion both these groups. The most traumatic event in her early life was the death of her little sister, aged eighteen months, when Olive was nine. Another emotional turning-point came when she read the Sermon on the Mount and realised that her parents 'did not *want* to live like that, although it was God's command which they professed to accept'. Like Waldo in the *African Farm*, she must have come to feel, 'I love Jesus Christ, but I hate God' (1).

As a very young but precocious girl she had already begun to formulate the questions which obsessed and tormented her in adult life. 'Why did everyone press on everyone and try to make them do what they wanted? Why did the strong always crush the weak? Why did we hate and kill and torture? Why was it all as it was? Why had the world ever been made? Why, oh why, had I ever been born?' These, she says, were her thoughts before the age of nine. But she cherished the hope that, somehow, things could be altered, 'I seemed to *see* a world in which creatures no more hated or crushed, in which the strong helped the weak'.[4] Although she had rejected her parents' faith, she kept the missionary temperament all her life.

In 1865 her father was dismissed and for the next few years Olive moved about between the homes of her elder brothers and sisters, helping in the house and later getting various jobs as a governess. Her family and friends thought her brilliant, but slightly mad. There were no secular or feminist movements in South Africa, but at quite an early age she had ceased to believe in God and developed her own, highly individual views on the position of women. Several of the people whom she cared about rejected her when she admitted to being a freethinker. 'All things on earth have their price', she noted in the *African Farm*, 'and for truth we pay the dearest. We barter it for love and sympathy' (2,1). She read Darwin, Spencer and Mill, and wrote a juvenile novel, *Undine*, which was not published until after her death. There was a brief engagement to a man of whom little is known, and after it ended she developed chronic asthma. By the time she was twenty-five she had had some bitter experiences and become convinced that women should support themselves rather than expecting a husband to solve all their problems. She had also, in the intervals between teaching, written *The Story of an African Farm* and an early version of *From Man to Man*.

Like many young women in the colonies, she believed she would have a richer life in England, and saved for years to pay her fare. Arriving in London in 1881, she began to send her novel round to publishers. It was finally accepted (by George Meredith, who had some sympathy with the feminist ideas it expressed) and came out in 1883, under the pseudonym of Ralph Iron. Its success was instant and lasting, although it was banned from some libraries. 'It is impossible to believe', wrote one reviewer, 'that . . . . the colonies will not fulfil the promise that is given by such a work of genius as *The Story of an African Farm*'.[5] For the rest of her life and beyond, she was known chiefly as the author of that novel.

For another woman, this could have been the start of a brilliant career. Yet somehow, now that she had got where she wanted to be, she frittered away the opportunity. Over the next few years she continued to work on *From Man to Man*, but it was never finished. She associated with little groups of freethinking intellectuals, groups with names like the Men and Women's Club and the Fellowship of the New Life. One of her closest friends was Marx's daughter Eleanor, whose relationship with Edward Aveling demonstrated to Olive how much an idealistic woman could be made to suffer by a certain type of man. Another was the writer Henry Havelock Ellis (1859–1939). They became very involved with each other and exchanged a series of letters, mostly about the relationship of men and women and how this could be reformed, but for some reason they did not marry.

Worn out by asthma and emotional crises, she came back in 1889 to South Africa, where she was something of a celebrity. 'I can't describe to anyone the love I have for this African scenery', she wrote, but at almost the same time, 'you don't know what Philistines the people in Africa are.'[6] Her feelings about the country of her birth remained ambiguous. In 1894 she married Samuel Cronwright, an ostrich farmer and keen politician who changed his name to hers. It was a happy relationship at first; afterwards tensions began to appear and they had to spend months apart, as Olive's asthma made it impossible for her to go on living in one place. His attitude to her – reverential but baffled – was summed up after her death:

> she was a woman of genius, so strange and incredible in her personality (I have often said I should not have believed beforehand such a person could be found) that I doubted whether it could be conveyed in writing.[7]

They had a baby girl, who died after one day. To her great sorrow, she was unable to have any more children.

Since the *African Farm* she had published nothing important; only *Dreams*, a collection of allegories, in 1890, and some stories and various articles on South Africa. *Trooper Peter Halket of Mashonaland*, a short novel attacking the policies of Cecil Rhodes, appeared in 1897. By the end of the decade her husband had begun to fear that she would never finish *From Man to Man*, the novel which she saw as her major work and which made the *African Farm* seem 'crude and youthful'.[8] When the South African War broke out they both threw themselves into campaigning for the Boers. The journalist H. W. Nevinson recorded his impression of Olive at an anti-war meeting:

> I have heard much indignant eloquence, but never such a molten torrent of white-hot rage. It was overwhelming. When it suddenly ceased, the large audience – about 1500 men and women – could hardly gasp. If Olive Schreiner (for, of course, it was she) had called on them to storm Government House, they would have thrown themselves upon the bayonets.[9]

She was kept under house arrest during the war, the Afrikaner village of Hanover where she was living surrounded by barbed-wire; before it was over, three local men had been executed. Afterwards, though, she became unpopular with the Boers whom she had championed, and showed great sympathy with the non-white South Africans. She resigned from the local women's suffrage league because it would not grant equality to black women. If the colour bar continued, she said in 1908, 'then I would rather draw a veil over the future of this land'.[10]

By this time she was chronically ill and saw little of her husband. Her novel remained incomplete. But in 1911 she published *Woman and Labour*, known to contemporary feminists as 'the bible of the women's movement'. It is a book which has dated very little, for she had a remarkably good idea of how life in the richer countries would develop. Women had always worked, she pointed out, but they could not go back to 'bearing water and weaving linen' in societies which were inventing more and more labour-saving machines, nor were they any longer expected to have enormous families. They would either have to go forward, and claim their share of the new kinds of work which were opening up, or become 'sex-parasites'. This meant a woman who did not work but simply attached herself to a man, a type she particularly despised. She argued that there was no reason why women could not be admitted to any profession, and that they might be better statesmen than men, because their special experiences made them particularly anxious to preserve life. 'No woman who is a woman says of a human body, "It is nothing!" . . . . She knows the history of human flesh; she knows its cost; he does not' (4).

In 1913 she went to England, without her husband, for medical treatment, and was trapped in Europe by the war. Her German name and pacifist sympathies made her life very difficult over the next few years. Afterwards Cronwright came to see her but, although they did not acknowledge this, the marriage had virtually broken down. He had supported the war; she thought it would produce evil 'for generations to come',[11] and there were other conflicts. She returned to South Africa alone, and died at a Cape Town boarding-house on 11 December 1920.

It is hardly possible to discuss Olive Schreiner's fiction without discussing her ideas. Her commitment to them led to tensions within her novels and contradictions in her personality. Believing totally in love and harmony, she found that political and religious differences led to estrangement from her family and friends. A childless woman, she loved children and believed there was no more important work than training the young. She was a feminist who had been hurt by men but did not reject marriage, writing that the ideal relationship was 'sexual companionship and an equality in duty and labour' (*Woman and Labour*, 3). The women in her novels never achieve this.

Her work has certain glaring faults. One is formlessness; *The Story of an African Farm*, for instance, pauses for a chapter while the Stranger tells a quite unnecessary parable about the White Bird of Truth. Again, *From Man to Man* is interrupted by the philosophical chapter 'Raindrops in the Avenue', and in both novels there are several other long interludes so that the characters can put the case for the author's ideas. Olive Schreiner was aware that some readers might find this habit annoying. She did it partly because she felt that the ideas were important and partly because, as she argued in her preface to the *African Farm*, she did not see it as her job to supply a perfectly-constructed plot:

Human life may be painted according to two methods. There

is the stage method. According to that each character is duly
marshalled at first, and ticketed; we know with an immutable
certainty that at the right crises each one will reappear and
act his part, and, when the curtain falls, all will stand before
it bowing. There is a sense of satisfaction in this, and of
completeness. But there is another method – the method of
the life we all lead. Here nothing can be prophesied. There is
a strange coming and going of feet. Men appear, act and react upon each other, and pass away. When the crisis comes
the man who would fit it does not return. When the curtain
falls no one is ready. When the footlights are brightest they
are blown out; and what the name of the play is no one
knows.

Believing as she did that there was no God and that the
universe lacked any obvious meaning, it was not possible for
her to write the old kind of novel in which the good are
rewarded, the evil punished, and every character has his or her
proper place. However, she still very much wanted to find
meaning in life. The philosophical discussions which interrupt
the action of the novels were, she believed, the core of them.
   Her other great fault, according to many people, is
sentimentality. She overworks the word 'little'; she overidentifies
with her heroines (as several other women novelists have done).
When, in *From Man to Man*, she interrupts a serious argument to
quote the jingle:

>   'Tis love that makes the world go round,
>   The world go round, the world go round!

it is easy to laugh. Certainly those who think that anyone who
wants to replace the present world order with a more humane
one is sentimental will have little time for Olive Schreiner. But
it should be pointed out that her ideas were derived not only
from Christianity and Socialism but also from her experience as
a woman; if she is sentimental, the average woman is too:

> 'It is a fine day, let us go out and kill something!' cries the
> typical male of certain races, instinctively. 'There is a living
> thing, it will die if it is not cared for', says the average
> woman, almost equally instinctively . . . . She always knows

what life costs; and that it is more easy to destroy than create
it. (*Woman and Labour*, 4)

'No literary record has been made by the woman of the past, of
her desires or sorrows', she wrote (*Woman and Labour*, 2). The
normal occupations of the women in her novels – housework
and child care – have, after all, always made up the greater
part of most women's lives. But, like the South African
landscape, they had not usually been written about.

'A striving, and a striving, and an ending in nothing' is the
author's motto for the second part of *The Story of an African
Farm*. The heroine, Lyndall, who is very similar to Olive, dies,
and although some people have found the last scene ambiguous
it surely means that Waldo dies too. The pessimism is typical of
late-Victorian novels. One reason why the *African Farm* appealed
so strongly to its first readers was that more and more people
were detaching themselves from traditional Christianity, often
with a good deal of pain. Some of them found aspects of it
morally repellent – the idea of hell, for instance, and also the
worldliness of many believers. Such people are savagely
caricatured in Bonaparte Blenkins's sermon, 'Let us not love too
much . . . let us think always of our own souls first' (1,5).

Reacting against the doctrine she had been taught as a child,
that 'the material world is but a film, through every pore of
which God's awful spirit-world is shining through on us', she
turned to nature and found it 'not a chance jumble; a living
thing, a *One*'. 'Nothing is despicable – all is meaningful,' she
proclaims in one of the many passages where she is speaking in
her own voice (2,1). Her novel made readers intensely aware of
the South African landscape which few of them had ever seen.
The 'karroo' or plain is apparently depressing, with its ants,
red sand and blazing heat. The ostrich farm is a place which
the more intelligent young people want to leave. But it does
produce forms of life which seem semi-divine; Waldo, in the
last chapter, considers the chickens as 'tiny sparks of brother
life', and has a feeling of reverence for the small ice-plant:

He loved it. One little leaf of the ice-plant stood upright, and
the sun shone through it. He could see every little crystal cell
like a drop of ice in the transparent green, and it thrilled
him.

Possibly the reason why Waldo is always lying on the ground is that he draws strength from the earth. It is quite common for sensitive people to turn to nature because they find human relationships too painful. Certainly, in this novel, they have little to offer. 'If the world was all children I could like it' says Waldo, 'but men and women draw me so strangely, and they press me away, till I am in agony. I was not meant to live among people' (2,11).

The child is always an important figure in Olive Schreiner's philosophy. The *African Farm* begins, like many great Victorian novels, with sensitive children being made to suffer by coarse and stupid adults. Lyndall resembles Maggie in *The Mill on the Floss* in being much more intelligent and morally aware than those who have charge of her. Apart from Waldo's father, the old German (whose childlike faith is quite unable to cope with evil), the adults are unsympathetic. They have no time for any books except the Bible and have not begun to come to terms with modern civilisation. 'When do we hear of Moses or Noah riding in a railway?' (2,14), asks Tant' Sannie. Both she and Bonaparte are very funny, but in Punch-and-Judy fashion; behind the knockabout humour their is terrifying violence. While Tant' Sannie is merely a stupid woman (although there is a suggestion that she devours her husbands), Bonaparte is an active sadist. His treatment of Waldo (scratching open his cuts with a fingernail, gratuitously breaking his machine) goes well beyond insensitivity and hints at the darkest forces in human nature. Between them they represent everything which will thwart any aspirations towards a better life.

In this novel the children never grow up. Lyndall and Waldo die in their teens or early twenties; Lyndall's baby lives for only three hours. There is nothing strictly logical about this pattern. On one level, of course, Lyndall dies because she breaks the rules and has a child, yet we last see Tant' Sannie enjoying rude health after *her* baby's birth. Whether or not a woman dies in childbirth surely has nothing to do with her moral qualities, nor is there any obvious physical reason why Waldo should die. It is implied, though, that young people who cannot adapt themselves to the cruelty of life will be crushed out of it. 'The young cut down cruelly, when they have not seen, when they have not known – when they have not found – it is for them that the bells weep blood' (2,12).

The theme has the same universal appeal as *Romeo and Juliet*, but Waldo and Lyndall are not lovers. 'We fight our little battles alone; you yours, I mine', the author comments. 'We must not help or find help' (1,9). They have surprisingly little to do with one another; the real tie between them is that 'we are both things that think' (2,6). But each worries about a different problem; Lyndall is not concerned with God or Waldo with feminism. It is perhaps fair to say that each of them represents a different aspect of Olive Schreiner.

Religion is Waldo's obsession. He feels isolated, and extremely wicked, because he cannot accept the faith of those around him and is too earnest to stop fretting about it. He tries sacrificing his mutton-chop and opening the Bible at random; both experiments fail and he ceases to believe in God. But his ethics, like the author's, are profoundly Christian. He refuses to avenge himself on Bonaparte; he suffers at the thought of all the 'countless millions of China and India' who are dying every moment of the day. 'Oh God, God! save them!' he cried in agony. 'Only some; only a few!' (1,1). This extreme, and some would say morbid, concern for others is shared by all the really 'good' characters in Olive Schreiner.

Like Waldo, Lyndall is eager to leave the farm and explore other possible ways of living; 'I like to experience, I like to try' (2,9). But, as she explains to him, she cannot knock about the world as he can; all women are expected to be under some man's protection. Over the next few years, several 'new women' appeared in English novels, including some who refused to get married. Lyndall was one of the first, and she had a profound effect on women readers (including, thirty years later, Vera Brittain). It is possible that her seduction by 'the stranger' was based on Olive's experiences as a young girl. The abstract ideas which Lyndall voices in her long speeches had almost certainly been worked out by the author herself.

The speeches may seem crude (and we may find it difficult to believe in Lyndall's fatal charm, which subdues every man she meets). But her tirade agains the oppression of women is still moving. 'I once heard an old man say, that he never saw intellect help a woman so much as a pretty ankle, and it was the truth' (2,4). She points out that from childhood females are trained, not to develop their talents, but to be pretty, polite and passive, so that they will stand a good chance of catching a man. Yet they will not get men's 'chivalrous attention' when they are old and faded. 'The bees are very attentive to the flowers till their honey is done, and then they fly over them.' Elsewhere men's love is compared to breaking butterflies. These ideas were to be developed at greater length in *From Man to Man*.

In the end Lyndall is broken, as she had half-expected. 'A little bitterness, a little longing when we are young, a little futile searching for work, a little passionate striving for room for the exercise of our powers – and then we go with the drove. A woman must march with her regiment. In the end she must be trodden down or go with it; and if she is wise she goes' (2,4). Em, who is a traditional woman and does march with her regiment, survives. But, like everyone else who meets Lyndall, she is affected by her example; whereas in the beginning she expects a great deal from marriage to Gregory, she ends up disillusioned. (Gregory himself is an unreal figure. His main significance seems to be that, while he talks about a 'man's right to rule' (2,10) on his first appearance, Lyndall forces him to rethink his views and he ends up, literally, 'unmanned'.)

Lyndall, and her creator, do not denounce marriage. Although Lyndall says that she is not in a 'hurry to put my neck beneath any man's foot' (2,4), the reason is that she has a high conception of a perfect union and will not accept anything less, even with the father of her baby. 'You call into activity one part of my nature,' she tells the man, 'there is a higher part that you know nothing of, that you never touch. If I married you, afterwards it would arise and assert itself' (2,9). The sadness of the novel is that this higher part of her nature never finds expression. She dreams of 'tunnelling mountains . . . healing diseases . . . making laws' (2,4), but this is impossible, and there is no suitable husband in sight. The baby, though illegitimate, evokes deeper feelings in her than any man has been able to do. 'Its feet were so cold; I took them in my hand to make them warm, and my hand closed right over them they were so little . . . . It crept close to me; it wanted to drink, it wanted to be warm' (2,12). Women who had borne children had not usually written books; before the twentieth century, it was unusual for these emotions to get into fiction.

'The souls of little children are marvellously delicate and tender things', says Lyndall, 'and keep for ever the shadow that first falls on them, and that is the mother's' (2,4). Unlike a later generation of feminists who tended to be hostile to motherhood, Olive Schreiner believed that it was one of the most important jobs that women could do, although they often did it badly under current conditions and although it should not prevent them from doing other kinds of work. At present everyone was suffering. 'Man injures woman', she wrote, 'and women injures man. It is not a case for crying out against individuals or against sexes, but simply for changing a whole system'.[12]

'It is only the made-up stories that end nicely', says Lyndall, and the *Story of an African Farm* reaffirms that individuals are doomed. The most they can hope for is to leave some imprint on their surroundings, like a book, or the bushmen's paintings. But the ultimate reality seems to be not God or the soul but the universe, which calmly contemplates the most searing human experiences, as Waldo realises in the scene under the stars or out on the karroo:

> Sometimes I lie under that little hill with my sheep, and it seems that the stones are really speaking – speaking of the old things, of the time when the strange fishes and animals lived that are turned into stone now; and the time when the little Bushmen lived here . . . . Now the Boers have shot them all, so that we never see a yellow face peeping out among the stones . . . . And the wild bucks have gone, and those days, and we are here. But we will be gone soon, and only the stones will lie on here, looking at everything like they look now. (1,2)

From Man to Man was published, posthumously and without a final chapter, in 1926. Perhaps because of its unfinished state, perhaps because Olive was firmly identified as the author of the *African Farm*, it got little attention, and was neglected for half a century until Virago reissued it in 1982. Yet it is a much better and more substantial book (though not faultless), and the basic situation is so fully worked out that the absence of a formal ending matters less than it might. Olive herself had no doubt that it was her best book. She spent years polishing and compressing it and perhaps was reluctant to let it go because she so much wanted it to be perfect. 'My one novel especially I would have liked so to finish' (she wrote in 1913, when she claimed that she was too ill to work). 'I feel that if only one

lonely struggling woman read it and found strength and comfort
from it one would not feel one had lived quite in vain.'[13]

The title is taken from a sentence of John Morley's, 'From
man to man nothing matters but charity'. A subtitle is *Perhaps
Only*, which may mean that *perhaps* we could have more humane
relationships if *only* we wanted them enough. The book was
dedicated to her little sister who had died as a child and to her
baby daughter – 'She never lived to know she was a woman'.
This was appropriate, because the central theme is the wastage
of potential.

Again, the story begins on a South African farm, but this
time a sheltered peach and fig farm which seems like paradise
after the two daughters have grown up and left it. Bertie, exiled
in England (which Olive portrayed as a dreary place where it
rains incessantly), remembers the mimosas 'beginning to burst
into their yellow blossoms ready for Xmas' (11); that single
detail makes us realise how much has been lost. It is a garden
of Eden invaded by a series of serpents (the tutor, Frank, John-
Ferdinand, Veronica), who are foreshadowed by the cobra
which Rebekah meets the day her sister is born. 'She had a
sense of all the world being abandonedly wicked; and a pain in
her left side' (Prelude). The girls will have to go out and be
destroyed by the evil in the world or fight it. Throughout the
novel, the image of the child who becomes a woman is central.

It is obvious that *From Man to Man* is about the deep love
between two sisters. Yet, like Waldo and Lyndall, they do not
really interact; each spends most of her time in 'the solitary
land of the individual experience' (*Story of an African Farm*, 2,4).
At the end of the 'Child's Day' they are sleeping in the same
bed, 'the arm of the elder sister so closely round the younger,
than she could not remove it without awakening both' (Prelude),
and the author planned to bring them together again at the end of
the novel when Bertie dies. In between, they rarely meet, have no
real conversations, and are practically unaware of each other's
problems. Rebekah's husband sees her as 'the type of all that
was pure and womanly' (8); Bertie, according to Cronwright-
Schreiner's notes, ends up in 'a house of ill fame . . . stricken
down by a loathsome and terrible disease'. The author's point
is that this is a false distinction; both 'good' and 'bad' women
are ruthlessly exploited by men.

The novel begins with a very basic experience, 'the agony of childbirth', when Rebekah's mother gives birth to twin girls, one living and one dead. Rebekah tries first to relate to the dead baby by giving it presents and then pretends to find her own baby in a mimosa-pod. Here again we see a child who is much brighter than those around her (the parents are nullities and the servants think she is mad), but it is clear that she is deliberately closing her mind to unpleasant facts. In the Prelude (which, her husband thought, 'is certainly almost wholly autobiographical'[14]), the little girl imagines a perfect world where children make friends with lions and tigers and where she teaches and takes care of her younger sister. When she says, 'You are killing it like the other one!' her facts are wrong, but her instinct that the baby is in danger does not mislead her. As we learn in the next chapter, leopards steal lambs, and the half-ripe peaches which fall into the grass and are eaten by pigs have a wider significance.

Throughout the book the younger sister is called Baby-Bertie because she never becomes fully adult. It seems her life is going to be that of the traditional woman, 'Bertie . . . got up before sunrise every morning to gather oranges and figs for preserves, and was busy all day making jams and almond cakes' (3). This kind of work is undervalued because it is done only by women, but it is necessary and can be deeply satisfying. Rebekah, herself a much more intellectual type, sees that if Bertie is allowed to be an ordinary wife and mother she will be safe:

> Some women with complex, many-sided natures, if love fails them and one half of their nature dies, can still draw a kind of broken life through the other. The world of the impersonal is left them: they can still turn fiercely to it, and through the intellect draw in a kind of life – a poor, broken, half-asphyxiated life . . . but still life. But Bertie and such as Bertie have only one life possible, the life of the personal relations; if that fails them, all fails. (3)

The significance of this for Rebekah herself becomes clear only halfway through the novel; in the early chapters we are concerned with Bertie. The powerful and painful narrative is very reminiscent of Hardy's *Tess of the D'Urbervilles*, although Olive Schreiner had certainly worked out the broad outlines of her story before she read it. Bertie loses her innocence at fifteen in an act of near-rape, then loses her fiancé John-Ferdinand when she confides in him. From then on there is very little for her. Like Tess, she is trapped between two incompatible demands – that she should be sexually available to any passing man and that a man's wife should be 'pure'.

Significantly, John-Ferdinand and Rebekah's husband Frank, who seem so different on the surface, are brothers. Frank is the average sensual man with the hunter's attitude – 'the woman who has once wholly given herself to you is a dead bird, a fish, through whose gills you have put your fingers' (8). John-Ferdinand is an Angel Clare-like figure, an admirer of the blameless King Arthur in Tennyson, a good man according to his lights. Yet because he is incapable of understanding the pressures on Bertie, he does her as much harm as the tutor, not only because he recoils from her and lets her see it but also because (influenced by his own high ideal of marriage) he tells her secret to his wife.

In case we are tempted to think that only men behave badly, Olive Schreiner gives us, in Veronica, a representative of pure evil. It is hard to say what motivates this outwardly good and respectable woman, who is not content with getting John-Ferdinand away from Bertie but is determined to see Bertie destroyed. Consider the scene where she finds her rival's picture:

> It was the portrait of a little child of four with a mass of brown curls about its head; the face was smiling; there were dimples in the cheek and in the chin; the child seemed bursting with life and joy . . . . Veronica looked down closely into the face, and her eyes contracted slowly at the inner corners. Quickly she put the case down open on the table, and, placing her large flat thumb on the face, she pressed; in a moment the photograph had cracked into a hundred fine little splinters of glass radiating from the face, which was indistinguishable.   (4)

It is not clear at first why this passage is so frightening; after all, destroying a photograph is not a major crime. But the point is that Veronica's malice has no motive; she hates Bertie and Rebekah simply because of what they *are*, and the horror is heightened by the fact that the photograph is not of the grown-up Bertie but of a four-year-old child. Olive Schreiner had obviously thought hard about the mystery of evil and had not been able to explain it satisfactorily. Rebekah also realises, when she is in trouble, that other people gloat for no obvious reason, 'it is like when wild animals gather round the wounded one of the herd and prod it with their horns' (8). This is what happens to Bertie, who is driven first from her sister's home and then from her aunt's by the gossip Veronica has set going. The chapter 'Cart Tracks in the Sand' shows her last attempt to find a place for herself within society. She has given up hoping for marriage and tries to fulfil her need for affection (and her creative urge) by cooking and sewing chair covers for her uncle and aunt. In the episode where she makes a frock for Veronica's baby, we are reminded that women who can express themselves in no other way have to do it through traditional 'women's work', 'The poet, when his heart is weighted, writes a sonnet . . . the publican and the man of business may throw themselves into the world of action; but the woman who is only a woman, what has she but her needle?' (9).

With all other options closed off, Bertie is more or less forced to elope with the nameless man known only as 'the Jew'. He is not a completely unsympathetic figure, but it is obvious there can be no real relationship between them. In the English episode Bertie (like the actresses in flesh-coloured tights) has become a 'sex-parasite'. Given what the man sees as ideal conditions – every luxury, no work or money worries – she finds that they are destroying her physically and emotionally. She has no outlet for affection (except the kittens), no freedom, no work and no money. The last two are important in the author's scheme of values; she believed, not only that idleness was damaging, but that women would never be able to control their lives unless they could find work and be paid for it. When Bertie is thrown out she inquires about a job, but is told she cannot get one without references. Ironically, Isaac brings her the money which would have given her a small measure of independence when it is just too late. This is the last we see of Bertie; her next step is open prostitution.

Several Victorian novelists had made the point that if the 'fallen woman' was not allowed back into society she would fall further, and Bertie's story, as a story, is not new. Rebekah is much more unusual. Perfectly respectable in sexual terms, she is actually a far more subversive thinker than poor Bertie who

only wants to be allowed to live. We first get to know the inner
life of the adult Rebekah in a chapter, 'Raindrops in the
Avenue', which is certainly too long, and which some critics
have found boring. 'The daughters of educated men have
always done their thinking from hand to mouth', wrote Virginia
Woolf, '. . . they have thought while they stirred the pot, while
they rocked the cradle.'[15] Rebekah does her thinking and writing
in between darning stockings and mixing the dough. She has a
great need to make sense of her own life, and life in general,
and the jottings in her notebook – which we should not skip –
form some sort of a reply to Olive's childhood question, 'Why
did the strong always crush the weak? . . . . Why was it all as it
was?' Going right back in history to the fall of Greece, she
points out that Greek civilisation had no firm foundation
because it excluded slaves and women, and women 'alone have
the power of transmitting the culture and outlook of one
generation safely to the next' (7). In fact, in the chapter,
'Fireflies in the Dark', we see Rebekah *teaching* her children,
rather than simply taking care of them; here she warns them
not to believe in superior and inferior races and tells them the
parable of the 'tall queen-lilies' who believe they are better than
all other flowers, 'We must reign here alone, all the others must
die to give place to us' (12).

In Rebekah's notebook, which we read before we know what
is happening to her marriage, she argues that all life is precious:

> The fittest has survived! Under water, half-buried in mud,
> only the outline of the jaw and two deep slit eyes show where
> the alligator lies . . . . The gazelle has come down to the
> water to drink and has been drawn in by the mighty jaw; the
> little monkey, delicate, quick, high-witted . . . has come too
> near, and the brown stump has moved and snapped it up;
> the human child has come to play upon the bank and
> disappeared . . . the creature survives. In the ages which
> have passed since it came into being, many fair and rare
> forms have existed and passed out of existence . . . . Much
> has escaped – but, oh, for that which in the long, long,
> ravening struggle of the ages, has not escaped from the strong
> jaw and the long claw and the poison bag!   (7)

'The strong jaw and the long claw and the poison bag' – we

remember Veronica's 'large flat thumb' squashing the photograph. Bertie is destroyed by the malevolence of those around her, and there are other, less direct ways of cutting off human potential. 'What of the possible Shakespeares we might have had, who passed their life from youth upward brewing currant wine and making pastries . . . stifled out without one line written, simply because, being of the weaker sex, life gave no room for action and grasp on life?' (7).

Rebekah's answer to conventional theories of evolution is to point out, quite accurately, that there can be no 'survival' without the caring work of females:

> You say all evolution in life has been caused simply by this destruction of the weaker by the stronger . . . . Neither man nor bird nor beast, nor even insect, is what it is and has survived here today, simply because the stronger has preyed on the weaker . . . . Through all nature, life and growth and evolution are possible only because of mother-love. Touch this, lay one cold finger on it and still it in the heart of the female, and, in fifty years, life in all its higher forms on the planet world would be extinct . . . . Everywhere mother-love and the tender nurturing of the weak underlies life, and the higher the creature the larger the part it plays. (7)

It becomes clear in the next chapter that Rebekah is a traditional woman, in that she has based her life on a loving relationship, and that she and her husband have values so different that they might as well be at separate stages of evolution. As she explains in the long letter which he declines to read, she has already tolerated repeated affairs and cannot take much more. She has been victimised in a different way from Bertie, but keeping the rules has not brought her any permanent happiness:

> Perhaps in the end it all comes to this – that the love and fellowship which we are taught to look to as our end in life, which compensates us for all that larger world of duties and actions, which we dream of from our earliest girlhood as that which is to consecrate our lives, means in the end only this – an hour's light, and then a long darkness; the higher the flame has leaped, the colder and deader the ashes. (8)

The letter is an agonising document. She has done everything she can to make Frank happy; she has invited his women friends to the house; she has, in traditional female fashion, blamed herself for being unable to satisfy him, 'I have sought, as a rat in a trap seeks a way of escape, to find out I was wrong and you were right' (8). It is clear that she is not trying to hold on to a man who does not want her, only asking to be treated as a reasonable human being. When Frank refuses to discuss their problem (patronising her as a 'tired little woman' who has 'silly little fancies'), she accepts, at last, that he lives in the world of blind amoral instinct which she hates and fears. His attitude to women is compared to his hunting of animals; once he has possessed any one, he despises her (consider the way he and his friends abuse Mrs Drummond); his own wife, after a few years' marriage, is only valued as a housekeeper: 'When a woman has borne four children and had several miscarriages, she's not just what she was when you married her' (8).

We may wonder if Rebekah, like other Schreiner characters, is to die, of sheer disillusionment, and she does at one point come very near suicide. However, she has already hinted that some women 'can still draw a kind of broken life' from 'the world of the impersonal' (3). She continues to look after Frank's house and to keep him comfortable, but without wasting any more emotional energy on the relationship. Unlike Bertie, she has a private space where she can retreat when necessary – the study and the tiny fruit farm. Olive, like Virginia Woolf, understood the importance of having 'a room of one's own'.

The book ends with a rather dull conversation between Rebekah and Drummond, the man she ought to have married. 'But, as they were situated' (the footnote says) 'a more intimate relationship was unwarrantable to such a woman as Rebekah; for her it was impossible to do anything which could degrade such a love; it therefore became inevitable that she must give up and leave the one man who she felt could be her life's close companion, and so they parted forever.' Drummond is the legal property of the woman who played her part in breaking up Rebekah's marriage, and most people would think her scruples overstrained. Yet, after we have read the book, we feel sure that this is the right ending. It is not only that a conventional marriage for the heroine does not seem appropriate; the author also wanted to stress the importance of returning good for evil. Rebekah adopts Sartje, the child of Frank's affair with a black servant, and this act is intended to be seen as a small sign of hope for the future:

> I made believe I built a high wall right across Africa and put all the black people on the other side . . . . I used to walk up and down and make believe there were no black people in South Africa; I had it all to myself.   (12)

but gradually she has realised that 'they were mine and I was theirs, and the wall I had built across Africa had slowly to fall down' (12).

Suffering is almost inevitable, in Olive Schreiner's world, for those who think and feel too deeply. 'The foremost branch which grows too far beyond its fellows must ultimately be snapped off' (7). The only happy couple in this book are John-Ferdinand and Veronica; all the men and women who damage others are comfortable, self-satisfied, and without remorse. But the hopeful thing about this novel is that Rebekah, unlike Lyndall, Waldo and Bertie, survives. According to the plan, she will last be seen in the vast and ancient karroo, bringing up her children alone and supported by the 'unutterable beauty of wild nature'.

Olive Schreiner remains a lonely and prophetic figure; 'the day will never come', she said, 'when I can be in the stream'.[16] She wrote one celebrated novel, yet, paradoxically, her best work has been greatly undervalued. She also wrote a famous non-fictional appeal for women, but it is her novels which really make us sympathise with women's condition. She is an intensely local writer whose work has spread far beyond South Africa ('we learn not merely of a backwater in colonial history but of the whole human condition', to quote the blurb of the *African Farm*). Strangest of all, although she was a very 'modern' woman who understood and welcomed the changes taking place in her lifetime, she keeps coming back to the most basic human emotions, and to a landscape untouched by civilisation. In the projected last scene of *From Man to Man* she appears to have been saying that, in the end, only woman and the land remain.

2
Edith Wharton

Edith Newbold Jones, who became one of the greatest of American novelists, was born in New York on 24 January 1862. Her parents, George Jones and Lucretia Rhinelander, belonged to the 'old' New York families which had been settled in America for nearly three centuries and had been prominent in public life (a great-grandfather had fought in the War of Independence). Most of their money came from real estate and, as one of Edith's friends was later to say, 'her life and its structure stood fast on a solid plinth of "private means"'.[17]

In the 1930s she looked back nostalgically on the world of her youth.

> Between the point of view of my Huguenot great-great-grandfather . . . and my own father, who died in 1882, there were fewer differences than between my father and the post-war generation of Americans. That I was born into a world in which telephones, motors, electric light, central heating . . . X-rays, cinemas, radium, aeroplanes and wireless telegraphy were not only unknown but still mostly unforeseen, may seem the most striking difference between then and now; but the really vital change is that, in my youth, the Americans of the original States . . . were the heirs of an old tradition of European culture which the country has now totally rejected.[18]

In old New York, the 'good' families knew each other well (everybody was somebody else's cousin), customs hardly ever changed and there were certain unbending rules. Good manners and financial honesty were compulsory. The gentlemen were 'men of leisure', stuck in a 'narrow groove of money-making, sport and society' (*The Age of Innocence*, 34); as for their wives, 'child-bearing was their task, fine needlework their recreation, being respected their privilege'.[19]

A solitary child (her two brothers were much older), she spent a great deal of time in her father's library reading and making up stories. Between the ages of four and ten she toured Europe with her parents and learned to speak fluent French, Italian and German. She was always grateful for having had this 'background of beauty and old-established order'.[20]

It will be clear enough that Edith was born into a society which offered her far more cultural opportunities (books, music, leisure, travel) than South Africa had given to Olive Schreiner. But New York seemed poor and barren after that first taste of Europe. She was to keep going back there, as often as family responsibilities allowed, until she finally made her home in Paris in 1911.

She was a shy girl, already regarded as too intellectual for her environment; her mother was cold and unsympathetic. Pushed out on to the marriage market (it was taken for granted that any woman who did not marry was a failure), she suffered two wounding blows. Her first engagement was broken off, probably by the young man's mother. Then she became friendly with a young lawyer called Walter Berry, who was expected to propose, but did not. These experiences were not of the kind to give her much confidence in men. But in 1885 she married Edward Robbins (Teddy) Wharton, a Bostonian thirteen years older than herself.

In her autobiography Edith said as little as possible about her husband, and the friends she acquired after she had become a famous novelist found it extraordinary that she had married him. All the evidence is that Teddy Wharton was a pleasant man who enjoyed travel and country life, like Edith, but confessed he was 'no good' on her 'high plane of thought'.[21] He had no job and no money, and was sometimes described in later years as trailing round after her like an equerry. Their honeymoon was a disaster, and, for the next twenty years, Edith probably had no sexual relationship with Teddy or anyone else.

We know only a limited amount about her early married life. 'I had as yet no real personality of my own', she wrote later.[22] Childless, and with no strong emotional or intellectual bond with her husband, she seems to have been thrashing around in

search of something to do. They went to Europe every year;
Edith read voraciously and became something of an expert on
gardens, house decoration and the eighteenth century in Italy.
After 1890 she began to publish poems and stories in the
literary magazines. But she says that she was unable to write
'clear concise English' until Walter Berry reappeared in her life
and helped her with a manuscript (*The Decoration of Houses*)
which was giving trouble. Berry (who never married) was to be
one of her closest friends until his death in 1927.

The strain of establishing a 'real personality' led to a nervous
breakdown and long periods of depression throughout the
1890s. They cleared up as her career prospered and as she
began to strike out for herself. 'For nearly twelve years I had
tried to adjust myself to the life I had led since my marriage;
but now I was overmastered by the longing to meet people who
shared my interests.'[23] She made friends with several writers,
including, after 1903, Henry James. In Europe and especially
Paris, her writing was a social asset, but not in New York:

> None of my relations ever spoke to me of my books, either to
> praise or blame – they simply ignored them . . . the subject
> was avoided as though it were a kind of family disgrace.[24]

Her creative work began with short stories, followed in 1900
by a novella, *The Touchstone*, and a historical novel, *The Valley of
Decision* (1902). But her first major novel, which caused
something of a sensation, was *The House of Mirth* (1905). It was
written against the clock, for serialisation in *Scribner's* magazine,
an experience which taught her to work hard and regularly.

Totally professional, she spent her mornings writing
(producing poetry and travel books as well as fiction) and led
an active social life for the rest of the day. She had had a
country house built in Lenox, Massachusetts, and took long
trips by car into the New England countryside, the setting of
Ethan Frome and *Summer*. She also motored over England and
the Continent with her husband, Henry James and others of
her many friends. 'Why must Mrs Wharton be treated as
royalty?' asked one of them, Percy Lubbock. 'None knew why,
but all were conscious that she must.'[25]

As her reputation grew, her marriage declined. Teddy
Wharton began to show signs of mental illness and Edith felt

that she had missed fulfilment as a person. 'I think she's never really been unlocked', said one acquaintance, 'and that most of her emotions have gone into her books.'[26] Few people knew that in 1908 she had plunged into an intense affair with Morton Fullerton, an American journalist living in Paris. It had no future. Divorce was legal in the United States, and quite common in some circles, but to women of Edith's background it was profoundly upsetting; her ambiguous feelings can be sensed in many novels. Fullerton (who, as she later found out, had been engaged to an unsuspecting young woman in America during the time he was involved with her) probably had no wish to marry her anyway. 'How a great love needs to be an open and happy love!',[27] she wrote to him, and in 1912, when the affair had been over for two years, she spoke of 'the miserable poverty of any love that lies outside of marriage, of any love that is not a living together, a sharing of all'.[28]

Around this time, Teddy admitted that he had speculated with Edith's money and kept a mistress. She tried for a reconciliation, but his behaviour grew worse and finally in 1913, with the support of all her friends, she obtained a divorce.

The house in New England was sold, and she settled in Paris. *The Custom of the Country*, which appeared soon afterwards, was recognised as one of her most powerful books. After August 1914 she threw herself into the French war effort. A natural organiser on the grand scale, she looked after Belgian refugees, found work for unemployed women, visited the front, edited the *Book of the Homeless* which contained work by the leading writers and artists of the day. The French government made her a Chevalier of the Legion of Honour. Her own work, inevitably, was put to one side, although she did find time to write the striking short novel *Summer* in 1916.

After the war she divided her time between a villa near Paris and another on the Riviera. She revisited the States only once, saying that there was not 'much left of the America she valued'.[29] There were several aspects of modern civilisation which she disliked – the 'business courses and skyscrapers'[30] of America, most contemporary novels, and the wireless and cinema, 'those two world-wide enemies of the imagination'.[31] But she remained physically and mentally active, writing, travelling, helping charities, entertaining friends. Her novel *The Age of Innocence* won the Pulitzer Prize, the first time this award had gone to a woman, and she was nominated for the Nobel Prize, but did not get it. There is a description, from the 1920s, of the 'European' Edith, 'elegant, formidable, as hard and dry as porcelain', but at times this image cracked to reveal 'a nice old American lady'.[32]

Edith Wharton died at her home in Saint-Brice-sous-Forêt on 11 August 1937. Her creative powers had never waned ('All Souls', one of her finest ghost stories, was written only a few months before her death), but on the whole her post-war work is inferior. She turned out a string of novels and short stories for the women's magazines, writing too fast in order to make money for her dependants and charities. She is remembered almost entirely for the novels that lie between *The House of Mirth* in 1905 and *The Age of Innocence* in 1920.

As a young writer, Edith was annoyed by 'the continued cry that I am an echo of Mr James'.[33] and even today she is sometimes written off as one of the great man's disciples. Her early novella *The Touchstone* (which, significantly, is about a woman novelist who is too great for the men around her) lapses at times into a slightly mannered style which does recall James:

> 'I may never see you again', he said, as though confidently appealing to her compassion.
> Her look enveloped him. 'And I shall see you always – always!'
> 'Why go then –?' escaped him.
> 'To be nearer you', she answered.   (2)

But Edith's mature work imitates no one and demands to be read on its own terms. Of course, the two novelists were personal friends and had much in common. They were both Americans who eventually settled in Europe and were fascinated by the differences in customs and culture between the old world and the new. The brilliant *Madame de Treymes* (1907) has quite obviously been influenced by *The American*, showing as it does a conflict between 'innocent' Americans and 'sophisticated' French people, and with its hero prevented from being happy by the hidden power of family and Church. But while James kept coming back to the theme of Americans adrift in the subtly corrupting atmosphere of Europe, most Wharton novels are set in her own country and evil comes from within American society itself. She is more accessible than James (her work reached a far wider public) and, while she freely acknowledged that he was the greater writer, she handled several areas of human experience that he did not touch.

She shared his bleak view of human relationships. There are few happy endings in her novels, and those which do take place are severely qualified. Like Fleda in *The Spoils of Poynton*, and many other James characters, her people can frequently only get their heart's desire by doing something which, in the last resort, is morally unacceptable. They have good instincts, but live in a corrupt society. The question is whether they should snatch boldly at what they want, or hold back.

The Touchstone (1900) has a good example of this kind of dilemma. Glennard can only afford to get married if he sells the letters of a deceased literary woman, who was in love with him, to a publisher. As a minor character points out, the letters 'belonged to the public' (6); the act of publishing them was not wrong in itself. What was wrong was to use them for his personal advantage, especially as this involved marriage with a younger, more desirable woman. For this reason he cannot tell his wife about it, and the marriage is permanently flawed.

Sanctuary (1903), a much weaker story, repeats the theme of integrity versus self-seeking. Lily Bart's dilemma over the stolen letters in *The House of Mirth* is of the same sort. If she uses them she will be acting in self-defence; indeed her only alternative is social extinction. The action is not criminal, but neither is it, to quote George Eliot, 'ideally beautiful'. In the same way, John Durham in *Madame de Treymes* is asked to buy off his prospective wife's family with a sum he can easily afford; Newland Archer in the first part of *The Age of Innocence* is tempted to break off his engagement and marry the woman he really desires. It seems simple, but is not; and the characters who do take what they want usually find that this does not bring lasting satisfaction.

Bunner Sisters, written in 1892, although not published until 1916, was Edith Wharton's first valuable work. A clear-sighted and compassionate study of the lives of two women who have almost nothing, it was not at all what the wealthy author might have been expected to write. But she seems to have known this shabby part of New York quite well, and it is a convincing story. If there is a moral, it is a grim one, 'I always think if we ask for more what we have may be taken from us' (3). But she understood that even the very poor need emotional satisfactions; both sisters have dreams of romance, symbolised by the yellow jonquils which seem so out of place in their world. Ann Eliza needs to cherish her younger sister; this leads to the gift of the clock which brings Mr Herman Ramy into their lives. The irony is deepened by the fact that she gives up her own potential happiness to Evelina, and Evelina is killed by it. Like the author, Ann Eliza loses her belief in 'the personal supervision of Providence' (12); she is denied even the small luxury of feeling emotionally at one with her dying sister and her future, in a job market which expects women to be 'not over thirty . . . and nice-looking' (13), is bleak. Obviously they would have been wiser to stay in the boring but safe environment of their little shop. But a Herman Ramy, unlovely as he seems to us, is irresistible to lonely women who have seen nothing better. The tragedy stems from this unwelcome and unalterable fact.

Edith Wharton never forgot that millions of people were leading lives as stunted as the Bunner sisters', although most of her work is set in a more gracious milieu. Her later novels can be just as cruel, and the weak, indecisive men in them may be more cultured and scrupulous than Mr Ramy, but are not of much more practical use. In her world sexual love almost always ends tragically, and we discover that 'the fair surface of life' is 'honeycombed by a vast system of moral sewage' (*Sanctuary*, 5).

Part of the problem, she believed, was the gap between rich and poor, and in *The Fruit of the Tree* she argued that wealth should be used responsibly. She was also concerned about the fact that men and women, at least in the society she knew best, had scarcely any common interests. A character in *The Custom of the Country* says:

> The average American looks down on his wife . . . . How much does he let her share in the real business of life? How much does he rely on her judgement and help in the conduct of serious affairs? . . . . Where does the real life of most American men lie? In some woman's drawing-room or in their offices? The answer's obvious, isn't it? The emotional centre of gravity's not the same in the two hemispheres. In the effete societies it's love, in our new one it's business . . . .

Isn't that the key to our easy divorces? If we cared for women in the old barbarous possessive way do you suppose we'd give them up as readily as we do? ... All my sympathy's with them, poor deluded dears, when I see their fallacious little attempts to trick out the leavings tossed them by the preoccupied male – the money and the motors and the clothes – and pretend to themselves and each other that *that's* what really constitutes life! ... money and motors and clothes are simply the big bribe she's paid for keeping out of some man's way! (15)

Men and women know very little about each other's lives, like the wife in the ghost story 'Afterward' who simply is not aware that her husband's business methods have caused a death. As clearly as Olive Schreiner, Edith saw that the rich women whom she moved among were 'sex-parasites'. It is not surprising that Olive herself wrote in 1912, 'Edith Wharton's *House of Mirth* is one of the most wonderful expositions of the degradation and evils of woman's present position in modern civilisation that any pen could produce'.[34] She got the idea for this novel when she was wondering whether it was possible to write anything about New York smart society which would be worth reading:

There is was before me, in all its flatness and futility, asking to be dealth with as the theme most to my hand, since I had been steeped in it from infancy .... The problem was how to extract from such a subject the typical human significance which is the story-teller's reason for telling one story rather than another .... The answer was that a frivolous society can acquire dramatic significance only through what its frivolity destroys. Its tragic implication lies in its power of debasing people and ideals. The answer, in short, was my heroine, Lily Bart.[35]

Looking back on this society, eighty years later, we may find it somewhat difficult to get our bearings. The central figure is brilliantly illuminated while those who whirl around her are much vaguer. How, for instance, do we measure the difference in status between Mrs George Dorset and Mrs Norma Hatch? (One clue is that divorced women revert to their Christian names.) Certain old New York families (the Dorsets, the

Trenors, Lily's aunt) are 'in'; others, like the Gormers and the Welly Brys, are on the fringes; still others, like Rosedale and Mrs Hatch, are considered vulgar but will probably get into 'good' society eventually because they are rich. And this is the real deciding factor, 'Bertha Dorset's social credit was based on an impregnable bank-account' (2,8).

Lily, with no money to speak of, can only hold her place in this society by being a 'sex-parasite' in a refined way. She has 'been brought up to be ornamental' (2,11); she is expected to do little services for her hostesses and to amuse the men. But she is twenty-nine (a great age for a heroine in those days), has been seen around for too long and fears that her beauty is fading. 'What a miserable thing it is to be a woman!' she says in the first chapter, '. . . we are expected to be pretty and well-dressed till we drop.'

At the beginning of the book she is trying to capture an uninspiring rich man – 'she must follow up her success, must submit to more boredom . . . all on the bare chance that he might ultimately decide to do her the honour of boring her for life' (1,3). Plenty of novelists had written about husband-hunting girls, but rarely with so much sympathy as Edith Wharton does here. She understands the strength of Lily's temptations, which are described almost sensuously: 'her bedroom with its softly-shaded lights, her lace dressing-gown lying across the silken bedspread, her little embroidered slippers before the fire, a vase of carnations filling the air with perfume' (1,3). Flowers are constantly used to define Lily; her inability to understand what things cost is shown in the early scene where she demands fresh flowers on the table; she is 'like some rare flower grown for exhibition' (2,13). She can do nothing remotely useful, but her beauty and weakness tug at our sympathy. And, as we gradually find out, she is more than an ordinary gold-digger; the reason she is still single is that she has never quite been able to make herself marry in cold blood.

This is precisely why she is vulnerable. Married women can do as they like (Bertha Dorset's affairs are notorious, but she is safe for as long as her husband tolerates her), but unmarried girls are expected to keep certain strict rules. Lily cannot even take tea in Selden's rooms without being punished for it. Her name has been linked with too many men; she has begun to be talked about and, as she says, 'the truth about any girl is that once she's talked about she's done for' (2,4).

It is possible for a woman to be a spinster like Gerty Farish and keep her self-respect, but Lily is closer to the norm: 'all her being clamoured for its share of personal happiness' (2,13). Once she has been 'talked about' she is more likely to be exposed to crude sexual advances from men like Rosedale and Trenor. It is significant that she falls into the latter's power because she has taken money from him without understanding that it is a gift; one more example of the American woman's inability to enter the 'masculine' world of business.

Lily realises from the first that she cannot survive unless she marries. The world is 'not a pretty place; and the only way to keep a footing in it is to fight it on its own terms – and above all . . . not alone' (2,7). But, flawed though she certainly is, not one of the men in the book is her equal. Selden, the 'hero' who is forever blowing hot and cold, is a particularly infuriating character. Although the author seems to think that he stands for something better than the pleasure-loving society where Lily is trapped, the fact is that he too hangs around the smart set and has had an affair with the nastiest woman in it. This makes his patronising attitude to Lily, and his shocked recoil when he thinks her a 'fallen woman', hard to take. Without being aware of it, he is involved in her downfall from the very beginning, when she is caught coming out of his rooms, to the end where she destroys the letters because they are his – and, as Rosedale says crudely, 'I'll be damned if I see what thanks you've got from him' (2,7).

It is possible to read the last scene as a tragedy, like so many of Hardy's stories, where two genuine lovers are separated by a series of misunderstandings. But most readers are likely to sympathise so strongly with Lily that they thoroughly despise Selden, and this in fact is how the earliest readers of *The House of Mirth* seem to have reacted. Lily's feeling for him is genuine; it saves her from some mean actions. But whatever Edith Wharton consciously meant to do, she made him come over as cold-blooded and shallow (like the principal men in her own life). This is the only kind of man her heroines can love, and as a result they fight their battles on their own.

Gradually, as Lily slips down the social scale (all the way

from Mrs Trenor's drawing-room to the milliner's workroom),
a real sense of values awakes in her. Most obviously, she
decides in the end not to blackmail Bertha Dorset, while
accepting that she owes nothing to 'a social order which had
condemned and banished her without trial' (2,11). Sewing hats
for rich women, she becomes aware of the 'under-world of
toilers who lived on their vanity and self-indulgence' (2,10)
(and who can survive in the labour market, while she can not).
And then there is her powerful feeling for the sickly Nettie and
her baby. Edith Wharton had little experience of children, and
was thought not to like them, yet it is surprising how often she
uses the figure of the child to judge adults' morality. (We
remember Undine's neglected son; the unborn children in
Summer and *The Age of Innocence*; the vast extended family in *The
Children*.) Lily's last conscious thought is of this child, who
makes her aware of the need for a 'real relation to life':

> She herself had grown up without any one spot of earth being
> dearer to her than another: there was no centre of early
> pieties, of grave endearing traditions, to which her heart
> could revert . . . . All the men and women she knew were like
> atoms whirling away from each other in some wild centrifugal
> dance: her first glimpse of the continuity of life had come to
> her that evening in Nettie Struther's kitchen.   (2,13)

'The continuity of life' – the need, especially as it affects
women, for a higher object than pleasure – is the theme of her
next novel, *The Fruit of the Tree* (1907), a disappointing, cliché-
ridden book. Like *Middlemarch* (the echoes of George Eliot are
hard to miss), the woman who has a sense of social responsibility
is contrasted with the woman who does not. Bessie cares only
about spending money and easily forgets the 'toilers' who have
produced it. Edith Wharton is slightly contemptuous of the
man who married this shallow creature when he could have
had Justine (and assumes, rather arrogantly, that once Bessie is
crippled she might as well die). His second marriage seems to
have a better chance because it is based on common interests
and because Justine is a sensible woman. But, as in her other
novels, the marriage does not work. His knowledge of Justine's
act (which is far from 'ideally beautiful') sours their relationship
permanently.

The Reef is much more impressive. It too is a novel about two kinds of women: 'ladies', who may lead emotionally arid lives but have an easy time in other ways, and women who must work for a living and are sexually exploited by men. Darrow, the anti-hero, is 'grateful to both for ministering to the more complex masculine nature, and disposed to assume that they had been evolved, if not designed, to that end' (3). Anna and Sophy are both women whom he likes to be seen out with. But Anna's natural setting is the chateau with its air of 'high decorum' (15); Sophy's the depressing, anonymous hotel, based on a real place where Edith had stayed with Fullerton. Later she said that 'I put most of myself into the opus',[36] and the later part of the novel is full of the pain of a woman who feels passionate sexual love for a man, and knows that he is her moral inferior.

Sophy is not a fully worked-out character but the author clearly sympathises with her. 'She had the excuse of her loneliness, her unhappiness', Darrow tells Anna, ' – of miseries and humiliations that a woman like you can't even guess' (29). Elsewhere he wonders if Anna's sheltered upbringing has not unfitted her for life. These are valid points, but Anna – unlike, say, Mrs Sellars in *The Children* – is not merely a narrow upper-class lady but a woman of great integrity and (in the good sense of the word) delicacy. 'I want you to know me as I am', she tells Darrow (11); she has an 'incorruptible passion for good faith and fairness' (30). This is why she does not continue to condemn Sophy who, after all, seriously loves Darrow; the two women have more in common than they think. Darrow, on the other hand, is a diplomat who is adept at using words to conceal his real feelings – or lack of them:

> 'Don't suppose I don't know what you must have thought of me!'
> . . . 'My poor child', he felt like answering, 'the shame of it is that I've never thought of you at all!'   (20)

Anna finally decides that she cannot live with a man whose sexual code differs so radically from her own. This is partly self-preservation (she has no answer to the question, 'And when she ceased to please him, what then?' [34]) and should not be seen as prudery. 'Certain renunciations might enrich', the author concludes, 'where possession would have left a desert' (35).

Edith Wharton had already suggested, in *The House of Mirth*, that Victorian values were becoming obsolete and that the future belonged to the men of money. In *The Custom of the Country*, this is the central theme. The Marvells are one of the first families of old New York – snobbish, honourable, scrupulous in their financial dealings and not wishing to make more money than they have. Their moral code already seems old-fashioned to many of their countrymen – they abhor divorce, 'pretend that girls can't do anything without their mothers' permission' (1), 'don't even like it if a girl's been *engaged* before' (9). But the new millionaires are joyously revolving 'about their central sun of gold' (14), and we are moving fast into the age of the consumer society and the sex goddess.

The Spraggs (like Mrs Norma Hatch) come from the West, employ a masseuse, are very rich but are excluded from the best society because they are thought to be vulgar. Undine, though, resembles the old-style American lady in being quite ignorant of business. '*That* was man's province; and what did men go "down town" for but to bring back the spoils to their women?' (4). She expects her father and then her husbands to supply her with all the things she wants – and her wants are insatiable:

> Presently her attention was drawn to a lady in black who was examining the pictures through a tortoise-shell eye-glass adorned with diamonds and hanging from a long pearl chain. Undine was instantly struck by the opportunities which this toy presented for graceful wrist movements and supercilious turns of the head. It seemed suddenly plebeian and promiscuous to look at the world through a naked eye, and all her floating desires were merged in the wish for a jewelled eye-glass and chain. (4)

Could there be a better description of the way in which artificial wants are created? Originally, Undine decides to marry Ralph Marvell, not because she actually likes him (we are carefully told that she does not find him attractive at their first meeting), but because she has been told that he is 'the best'. The author wastes no time on the details of their courtship, merely tells us, which is all we need to know, that Undine has got her engagement ring and that it is the best of its kind.

However, it is obvious even before the wedding that her morality and the Marvells' are going to clash. Coming from a culture where 'such scissions were almost painless' (10), she innocently speaks her mind on divorce:

> I guess Mabel'll get a divorce pretty soon . . . . They like each other well enough. But he's been a disappointment to her. He isn't in the right set, and I think Mabel realises she'll never really get anywhere till she gets rid of him.   (7)

She is immediately told that a divorced woman is at a social disadvantage (as indeed she is, unless she marries again) and by the time she wants a divorce herself she has learned to employ a more refined vocabulary − 'I'm unhappy at home', 'born sensitive', 'a mother's feelings'. She enjoys playing a 'pure woman' with the artist Popple (14), and seeing herself as 'the wife of a celebrated author' (20) (after she has stifled all the creativity in Ralph). But once it is clear that Ralph is not able to give her all she wants she transfers her affections to her masculine counterpart, Peter Van Degen. Undine is the ultimate 'sex-parasite'.

The Custom of the Country appeared in the year of Edith Wharton's own divorce and, in this novel and others, she demonstrated that she knew exactly how painful a bad marriage could be. Yet she sympathised with the attitude of old New York, which found divorce disgusting. In an early story, 'The Other Two', she had described a thrice-married woman as being like 'a shoe that too many feet had worn'.[37] This woman has adapted herself to each husband to such an extent that she has no personality of her own; Undine, too, has no real thoughts or feelings (no wonder the sophisticated French find her boring) except the wish to have the best of everything. This is expressed by the fact that all her private dramas are played out before an audience − from 'Says Husband Too Absorbed in Business To Make Home Happy', through 'New York Beauty Weds French Nobleman' to 'American Marquise renounces ancient French title to wed Railroad King'.

These headlines are the most offensive aspect of the case to Ralph Marvell, feeling as he does that 'the coarse fingering of

public curiosity had touched the secret places of his soul' (23).
But Ralph, as Edith Wharton shows with considerable
sympathy, is a survival, 'stumbling about in his inherited
prejudices like a modern man in medieval armour' (25). His
training has not equipped him to defend himself in the ruthless
world of business; he cannot handle money, and he has failed
to ask for custody of his son because this would have been
distasteful. 'He recalled all the old family catch-words, the full
and elaborate vocabulary of evasion: "delicacy", "pride",
"personal dignity", "preferring not to know about such things"'
(32). Finally, in his encounter with Moffatt, the old sensibility
and the new clash head-on with disastrous results:

> 'Look here, Moffatt', he said, getting to his feet, 'the fact that
> I've been divorced from Mrs Marvell doesn't authorise any
> one to take that tone to me in speaking of her'.
>   Moffatt met the challenge with a calm stare under which
> there were dawning signs of surprise and interest. 'That so?
> Well, if that's the case I presume I ought to feel the same
> way: I've been divorced from her myself'.   (35)

Reticence, chivalry, monogamy – the whole 'archaic structure'
of Ralph's emotions comes crashing down, and his breakdown
and suicide are most movingly portrayed. It is convincing that
he finally shoots himself because he cannot face having to speak
to the servant.

It seems to be an example of Undine's good luck that this
should happen exactly when she wants to make a Catholic
marriage. The fact that she has yet another husband living
simply does not enter her consciousness: 'As to her earlier
experiences, she had frankly forgotten them' (37). Henry James
thought that Edith had said too little about Undine's French
marriage, and that the novel should have concentrated on the
theme 'of a crude young woman . . . entering, all unprepared
and unperceiving, into the mysterious labyrinth of family life in
the old French aristocracy'.[38] That, however, was not her main
interest. She took pleasure in showing the peculiarities of French
society, as they appeared to Americans; she even makes us
sympathise with Undine when she has to endure French
mourning, 'encircled by shrouded images of woe in which the
only live points were the eyes constantly fixed on her least

movements' (38). But, in spite of great differences, the aristocracies of France and of old New York do have some common qualities. Ralph and Raymond are merged in Undine's mind because they are both chivalrous gentlemen. Both of them irk her when she is actually married to them because they value certain things – family, tradition, good breeding – above money. In each case she leaves her husband for a cruder man who seems able to offer her all the consumer goods she desires.

Obviously her real soul-mate is Moffatt who, like Rosedale in *The House of Mirth*, begins as a rank outsider but eventually gets to the top. Again like Rosedale, he is by no means the worst person in the book; compared to Undine he seems a fairly decent human being (though a 'shadowy destructive monster' [18] in public life). But although she will probably stay married to him, she is not content, 'She had everything she wanted, but she still felt, at times, that there were other things she might want if she knew about them' (46). When, on the last page, she discovers that she can never be an Ambassador's wife, this naturally turns out to be the one thing she really wants. An eyeglass or an Ambassadorship – there will always be something just out of her reach.

The novel, then, is a comedy, but a distinctly dark one; we cannot merely laugh at Undine when we read the slow painful chapters about Ralph's decline or see, at the end of the book, what her lifestyle has done to her child. Even Undine herself, at one point, evokes sympathy, for she does not progress smoothly from one marriage to the next but has a 'bitter two years of loneliness and humiliation' (37) when Van Degen leaves her. Women, it seems, are still the more vulnerable sex and must fight for their lives in the marriage market as the men do on Wall Street. In the end, their choice is to be an Undine or a Lily Bart. The Moffatts and the Van Degens have the real power.

While she had little sympathy for the artificial wants of rich women, Edith Wharton did sympathise intensely with people who had almost nothing and who instinctively reached out for a fuller life. The two short novels *Ethan Frome* (1911) and *Summer* (1917) continue the theme of *Bunner Sisters* and appear to have the same grim moral – that if you try for love or passion you could make your situation much worse. They are generally printed together and the author referred to *Summer* as 'the hot

Ethan'. Both are set among New England villages 'still bedrowsed in a decaying rural existence, and sad slow-speaking people living in conditions hardly changed since their forbears held those villages against the Indians'.[39] Earlier lady novelists, she felt, had described them much too sentimentally.

Ethan Frome takes place in a snowy landscape among limited and sluggish people – 'most of the smart ones get away' (1). Ethan himself has always wanted something better; he is interested in astronomy and biochemistry; he would like to live in a town. But he is compelled to scratch a living from the land and to contemplate his own name on a tombstone, perpetually joined with 'Endurance his wife'. Endurance, of course, is a central theme.

We find him married to a woman whose main interest is her own bad health (did she become ill because she was bored?) and whose only really passionate feelings are about her pickle-dish. It is natural that he yearns for Mattie as 'a bit of hopeful young life' (1). Divorce does cross his mind but, as in other Wharton novels, it is a legal, not a moral possibility. One reason why he cannot leave is the want of fifty dollars; Edith Wharton was always aware of the 'hard compulsions of the poor' (10). But, worse, Ethan is chivalrous to the core, believes that neither of the two women can survive without him, and must let one of them down. A romantic death-pact seems to be the only answer.

But now we see the reason for the time-lag, which several critics found irritating. Up to the last few pages, the author has allowed us to think that Mattie was killed in the accident. In almost all novels, the heroine is incorruptible, even if the most she can get is a beautiful death like Lily Bart. We are unspeakably shocked when we meet the whining invalid whom Mattie has become. 'I never knew a sweeter nature', a friend explains, 'but she's suffered too much' (10). Ethan comes over as a stronger character, who has retained some dignity and self-respect. But he must live with the knowledge that Mattie's suffering was caused by his attempt to break free.

Summer, though it lacks the tremendous impact of *Ethan Frome*, is possibly a greater novel. Certainly, by the time she wrote it, Edith Wharton had begun to feel that the New England villages might have some positive aspects after all. Not that North Dormer is in any way romanticised. It has no shops, railways, or cultural life; the people are mean and they gossip; even the library is not an outpost of civilisation but a dusty prison for a young girl on a June day. Her natural reaction is 'How I hate everything!' (1). But although she plans to get away, Charity is intensely sensitive 'to all that was light and air, perfume and colour . . . . She loved the roughness of the dry mountain grass under her palms, the smell of the thyme into which she crushed her face' (2). She is obscurely pained when a man puts his muddy boot on the white bramble-flowers. In other words, she is making the transition from child to woman, and the man who will deflower her has already appeared.

Charity is no meek victim but a tough young woman, descended from the lawless Mountain people, and one who knows what will happen if she gets pregnant. She has already dealt quite competently with Lawyer Royall (and this early incident has fixed him in the reader's mind as a dirty old man). She is less able to be sensible about Lucius Harney, who has the attraction for her that a 'city fellow' always does have for rural girls – 'almost every village could show a victim of the perilous venture' (5). Although he has everything that Lawyer Royall does not – youth, good looks, smooth manners – we never doubt that he will marry a girl of his own class. He and Charity speak different languages; compare her honest and straightforward letter to him with his to her, 'so beautifully expressed that she found it . . . difficult to understand' (15). Charity does not expect very much from him and the reader is not expected to feel much resentment towards him; he is merely a rather 'soft' young man behaving like the other young men in his group. Charity knows that she is the stronger of the two, but ultimately cannot defend herself against an irresistible force.

This force is, first, the summer, which briefly makes the landscape beautiful, then the passionate excitement in Nettleton, the local big town, on the Fourth of July. Charity, who has hardly ever been out of North Dormer, is assaulted by a flood of sense-impressions – crowds, fireworks, jewellers' windows with their 'hidden riches', 'drug-stores gushing from every soda-water tap . . . fruit and confectionery shops stacked with strawberry-cake, coconut drops, trays of glistening molasses candy' (9) – and so on. Each experience succeeds the next in an orgy of mass emotion and lavish spending, culminating in the

first kiss. But in the midst of it she gets a glimpse of Dr
Merkle's abortion clinic, and this reminds us, if not her, that
women cannot separate sex from its consequences.

She ceases to live for the moment, and grows up, once she
knows that she is responsible for her baby's future. Rejecting
Dr Merkle's deadly attentions, she seeks out her mother, who
after all had once tried to get a better life for her. But her
mother is dead; the choice seems to be prostitution, or the
spiteful remarks of North Dormer. She can only re-enter society
if she has the protection of a man.

That Lawyer Royall should turn out to be compassionate,
trustworthy, and prepared to bring up another man's child
will certainly surprise some readers – the author has gone out of
her way to draw attention to his faults. But her more attractive
heroes (Lucius, Selden in *The House of Mirth*) have a habit of
not being around when the heroine needs them. Precisely
because Charity has learned to limit her expectations, she has a
reasonable chance of a marriage that works.

Lawyer Royall's speech, about coming home to North Dormer
'for good', is a touchstone. By the end of the book we realise
that, after all, there are worse places – the Mountain, obviously,
and perhaps New York where Lucius has his club and where
Edith Wharton had set several stories of betrayal. It is clear,
anyway, that Charity could never have lived there with him.
She does not want to deny the experience (this is why she
retrieves the blue brooch) but passion is no more typical of life
than the Fourth of July is of the rest of the year. This is one of
the few Wharton novels with a 'happy ending', and,
characteristically, the happiness is limited.

The last of her great novels, *The Age of Innocence*, was set in the
vanished New York of her youth, which she carefully
reconstructed like 'the recovered fragments of Ilium' in the old
Metropolitan Museum (31). It had quite gone by this time, and
had been almost transformed by social and technological
changes – 'long-distance telephoning . . . electric lighting and
five-day Atlantic voyages' (34) – when the novel ends in about
1905. However many other things she is doing, the author
never ceases to be aware that she is describing the manners and
morals of a small closed society at a particular point in time:

'It seems cruel' she said, 'that after a while nothing matters

... any more than these little things, that used to be necessary and important to forgotten people, and now have to be guessed at under a magnifying glass and labelled, "Use unknown"'   (31)

Even passion, like everything else, is subject to the law of change.

The novel could be read as the story of a man who is too timid to grasp what he really wants, has a conventional marriage with a limited woman and ends up a 'mere grey speck of a man' (34). This would not be quite accurate. Old New York *is* limited; it is indifferent to the arts and afraid of other ways of life; its 'innocence' is in part 'the innocence that seals the mind against imagination and the heart against experience' (16). Its treatment of women is particularly open to question. In a famous, and slightly later story, 'The Old Maid',[40] set in the 1850s, a woman who has had an illegitimate baby is forced into celibacy; it is inconceivable, even to the kindest members of her group, that she could be allowed to get married. When her daughter grows up it seems that she too will 'fall' because no one is willing to marry a girl of unknown background. Her aunt adopts her, giving her a name and an income, after which the man agrees to marry her, and this is supposed to be a happy ending.

It is this double standard which leads a fairly enlightened young man like Newland Archer to say, 'Women ought to be free – as free as we are' (5). And when Mrs Mingott says that Ellen's 'life is finished' (17) because she has made an unhappy marriage, we share his recoil. But the double standard is not confined to old New York; woman is 'the subject creature' (31) in every country. Ellen, like Fanny in *Madame de Treymes*, has married into the European aristocracy and acquired a sophistication which makes American women seem 'curiously immature' (8). But we are given to understand that her life has been so horrible that it cannot be described directly. 'Intolerable, past speaking of, past believing' (13), is as much as we are ever told.

Archer constantly finds himself criticising May (whose parents' way of life is particularly vapid) because she is the product of a society which carefully ignores anything 'unpleasant'. 'Generations of the women who had gone to her making had descended bandaged to the family vault' (10). The question we are asked to consider is whether it is better for girls to be brought up in ignorance or to get experience at Ellen's price. There seems to be no middle way.

To Archer, dissatisfied with his little world and knowing exactly what he will get if he marries May, Ellen – detached, unshockable, familiar with alien countries and cultures – represents new possibilities. Their unconsummated love is expressed in terms of long silences and snatched meetings, boats, 'a wide space of water', 'a fresh world of ruffled waters, and distant promontories with lighthouses in the sun' (21, 23). They are separated not just by Archer's marriage but by the whole physical and moral gulf between America and Europe, a Europe which, as in James' novels, is dazzling, splendid, pervaded with great art and old traditions – and fundamentally corrupt.

On his wedding journey, Archer meets some Europeanised Americans – 'queer cosmopolitan women, deep in complicated love-affairs which they appeared to feel the need for retailing to everyone they met' (20); this is one hint that the 'European' woman is not to be seen as the ultimate value. Again, when he compares May and Ellen, it is usually to the latter's advantage, yet he notes that one cannot imagine May 'hawking about her private difficulties and lavishing her confidences on strange men' (11). Reticence and dignity, the 'dim domestic virtues' (11) of old New York, do count for something, and we are constantly having to balance them against its obvious faults.

Without fully believing in it, Archer describes the morality of his group to Ellen in 'stock phrases':

> The individual, in such cases, is nearly always sacrificed to what is supposed to be the collective interest: people cling to any convention that keeps the family together – protects the children, if there are any.   (12)

Ellen comes to believe these 'stock phrases', which represent the things she most values in New York culture – 'things so fine and sensitive and delicate that even those I most care for in my other life look cheap in comparison' (24). Like Maggie in *The Mill on the Floss* (although this plot is considerably more subtle), she will not let him break off his engagement to another woman who happens to be her cousin. The author does not question her right to get a divorce, only her right to damage others, and as Ellen points out (18) 'right' in this context can be an 'ugly word'. Once May and Archer are actually married, the ugliness becomes more serious. He dreams of going to Japan, but there is no country in the world where they can be together openly and honourably. Deceiving a wife is more serious than deceiving a husband because the woman is more vulnerable, and the 'masculine solidarity' (31) which conceals an affair is repellent to them both. Finally, the 'children, if there are any' become the real child whom May is expecting. After this has been revealed, it is clear that the relationship must end.

The long last chapter, which vastly enriches the novel, puts Archer's life in perspective. The world is changing, in some respects for the better, and he has done his part as a 'good citizen' (the phrase is new since his youth) and a solid family man. He acknowledges that 'there was good in the old ways'. His marriage has not been perfect, but then marriages, in Wharton novels, never are. His children 'take it for granted that they're going to get whatever they want', but he remains 'old-fashioned' and walks away from Ellen, although she is the one woman who really counts for him, because he has chosen to live by 'American' values and the two civilisations will not merge.

In spite of much inferior work, Edith Wharton is one of the great women novelists. Indeed, she produced more good work than there is room to discuss here; readers must discover her many superb short stories ('Roman Fever', 'Pomegranate Seed', 'Kerfol', 'The Eyes') for themselves. She described, better than any other novelist (not excluding James), what was happening to old-fashioned America in her lifetime and, as her biographer says, her work is 'quiet, continuing testimony to the female experience under modern historical and social conditions, to the modes of entrapment, betrayal and exclusion devised for women in the first decades of the American and European twentieth century'.[41]

3

F. M. Mayor

Of all distinguished English novelists, Flora Macdonald Mayor has perhaps been the least valued. In her lifetime – although she was never famous – she was compared with Jane Austen and Mrs Gaskell, and this was not ridiculous. Her sensibility is a modern one, and her best work was written after the First World War, but she belongs to the great tradition of nineteenth-century women novelists. Her two novels, *The Third Miss Symons* and *The Rector's Daughter*, have recently been reprinted, but before the 1970s she was almost unknown, and in most literary histories she is not mentioned.

She was born on 20 December 1872 into a comfortable home in Kingston-on-Thames. Her father, the Reverend Joseph Mayor, was Professor of Classics and later of Moral Philosophy at King's College, London. Two uncles were fellows of Cambridge colleges and her mother, Jessie Grote, was the niece of Professor George Grote, the historian of Greece and co-founder of London University. Women in her family were encouraged to use their minds; Mrs Mayor was a brilliant linguist and had translated the Icelandic sagas into English. The children grew up in an 'atmosphere of scholarship and refinement'.[42]

Both parents were in their forties and there were seven unmarried aunts, born before the accession of Queen Victoria, who helped to bring up the Mayor children. This gave them a living link with an age that had gone. Flora had a happy childhood with her twin sister Alice, her closest friend throughout life. They were carefully educated at a church high school and in Switzerland. At the age of twenty she went, without Alice, to Newnham College, Cambridge.

One reason why she eventually did so much more with her life than her sister was, perhaps, that she had those stimulating

42

years at university while Alice remained at home. She met a number of interesting women and made contact with unfamiliar ideas. She read her 'first definitely Unchristian book' – *The Story of an African Farm* – which, her father warned her, was 'not in the least the book for young and thoughtless girls':

> You will probably meet people of advanced views at Newnham, and some of our friends thought we were rash in letting you go there, but it is no longer possible for women to go through the world with their eyes shut.[43]

Flora did not break with her parents' values but neither did she continue the family tradition of scholarship. A plain but lively girl, she had a 'rapturous' social life (although there is no record of any boy friends at Cambridge; at least one man called her 'common and flippant').[44] After a happy career of socialising, light reading and amateur dramatics, she came away with a Third in history.

She returned to Kingston to join Alice as a 'daughter at home'. Young ladies did not do housework in those days but they were expected to fritter their time away paying calls, entertaining aged aunts, playing tiddleywinks, organising church bazaars, and so on. It is possible to exaggerate the boredom of their lives; the Mayors were more enlightened than many parents and both girls met men and received proposals of marriage. But Flora soon began to find it intolerable. She fought hard to break away but, as it turned out, almost all the rest of her life was spent under the same roof as one or other member of her immediate family.

Over the next few years she played with the ideas of writing and of becoming a professional actress. She wrote a novel, *Mrs Hammond's Children*, which was published in 1901 under the name of Mary Strafford, and was not a success. Acting was a more serious interest when she was in her twenties. She answered advertisements, hung around theatrical agents, even paid to be a 'walker-on'. But everything was against her. Her family were distressed that she should wish to do such unladylike work; she had to use a stage name ('Mary Strafford' again) and, even thirty years later, her brothers and sister refused to talk about this episode in her life. Her looks and background hurt her chances; so did the fact that she would have objected to acting in plays she thought immoral. She got very few parts.

By 1900, at the age of twenty-eight, she feared she was 'beginning to be a laughing stock'.[45] It is interesting that, like Olive Schreiner, she developed asthma as a young woman and was tormented by it for the rest of her life. It could have had a physical cause; it could also have been triggered off by emotional strain. She was clearly failing in her personal and professional life, but the experience did no harm to the future novelist. She was discovering a world very different from that in which she had grown up, and – this is a basic theme in her novels – was suffering a long series of humiliations and rejections.

Early in 1903 she was doing her first provincial tour, tramping the streets for lodgings and being appalled by the squalid conditions in theatres, when an old friend came to Macclesfield and asked her to marry him. Ernest Shepherd was a young architect without an income, much loved by the students at Morley College for Working Men and Women whom he taught for nothing. He had wanted to propose to Flora for some time, but had had to wait until he got a job. Now he told her that he had an appointment on the Architectural Survey of India. They became engaged and Flora gave up the stage for good.

They had about a month together before Ernest sailed for India. Years later, Flora said that if it had not been for Alice she would have gone with him 'and might have had my baby'.[46] But the marriage was put off for nine months, to give her sister time to get used to the idea, and in October, as Flora was preparing to leave England, she heard that Ernest had died of fever.

This was her one love affair, almost as brief as Mary's in *The Rector's Daughter*. She collapsed and was ill for months with asthma and heart trouble; indeed, she remained a semi-invalid for the rest of her life. In the following year she wrote in a diary:

> What on earth am I to do all day? . . . Up to the afternoon of Thursday Oct 22 when Mr Marshall's telegram came, I instinctively put happiness as what I was aiming for and expecting as my right in life. Since then I have also quite instinctively given up expecting it and also aiming for it; it seems absurd to aim for it when I see no prospect of getting

it. That means . . . really my whole outlook on life is changed,
and yet here one goes on outwardly absolutely the same.[47]

In spite of her clerical background, she had been virtually an
agnostic at the time Ernest died. Now she found that 'Christian
hope failed her not for hours and days, but for weeks and
months'.[48] Gradually she did recover her early religious beliefs.
But her outward life remained deadly dull. Too frail to get
regular work, she lived between 1904 and 1911 with her brother
Henry, a classics master at Clifton College, Bristol, and then
with another brother in London until his marriage in 1913. She
saw her friends, took an interest in women's suffrage, and in
1913, the year she moved back to live with her elderly parents,
published her first major novel, *The Third Miss Symons*.

'Major' might seem the wrong word for so short and
unpretentious a book, but it was well reviewed and very nearly
won the Polignac Prize. There were to be no more novels for
some time, partly because of Flora's bad health and partly
because of the demands on her during the war years. Much of
this time was spent helping her brother, now a housemaster at
Clifton, 'having to allocate beds in a schoolboys' dormitory and
make unpopular decisions about their jam ration'.[49] She felt
wasted in this job, and was not generally liked. 'Our failure is
so hard', she wrote to Alice, 'and so undeserved.'[50] In 1919 she
gave it up for good and began work on her masterpiece, *The
Rector's Daughter*. The theme had been suggested by the death of
an older friend, Mary Walton, who lived, unmarried, at Little
Shelford near Cambridge. She had spent years looking after
difficult elderly relations. 'I always do feel the stagnation here',
Flora had written, 'and I do feel very much the sadness of
Mary's wasted powers.'[51]

She had trouble finding a publisher; perhaps, after the war,
this story about an Edwardian spinster seemed hopelessly
dated. In 1924 Leonard and Virginia Woolf offered to publish
it at the Hogarth Press on a commission basis. It sold reasonably
well and was admired by several critics and readers, including
E. M. Forster. But Flora Mayor was not productive enough,
and perhaps not sentimental enough, ever to be a best-seller.

Her last years – spent with her mother in Kingston and, after
her mother's death, with Alice in Hampstead – were a time of
physical and intellectual decline. The sisters lived off their

dividends and Alice nursed Flora through constant attacks of asthma. She wrote one more novel, *The Squire's Daughter* (1929), which is nothing like as good as her earlier work. In some ways she had become the kind of sour old reactionary whom she had painted with some amusement in *The Third Miss Symons*; she felt that most of the English traditions she valued were on the way out. She also left some stories which were published posthumously in *The Room Opposite* (1935). She died at Hampstead on 28 January 1932, of pneumonia complicated by influenza. The Poet Laureate, John Masefield, an old friend and admirer, wrote an obituary note, but *The Times* refused to print it, and her work was forgotten for the next forty years.

Flora Mayor's two novels – for there are only two, one of them very short, which matter – have essentially the same subject. Each is about a spinster, moulded by Victorian ideas, who has no personal fulfilment, lingers on to be despised by the bright young moderns, and eventually dies. Each novel, in its own way – for the women have completely different personalities – asserts the value of their lives.

Old maids have traditionally been an object of ridicule. By 1913, when *The Third Miss Symons* was published, there were more of them than ever before. Women have always outnumbered men (the Great War made the problem even more painful) and, for much of the nineteenth century, middle-class girls were not expected to work outside the home. Some of the women who did not marry became philanthropists, novelists, travellers or suffragettes. Many more had wasted lives, staying with their parents until middle age or death and achieving nothing in their own right.

A perceptive reviewer said that F. M. Mayor was 'in the tradition, though her performance is not yet on the level of Jane Austen and Mrs Gaskell'.[52] Understandably, women writers had always shown more sympathy for old maids than had the men. But they did not often put them at the centre of their canvas; the tradition that novels should have a 'happy ending' was too powerful. Jane Austen showed only one real spinster, Miss Bates, who, as she pointed out, was likely to be snubbed cruelly by the young and successful. However, *Persuasion* (which, Flora Mayor said, 'had influenced her rendering of the emotional life more than any other work'[53]) and *Mansfield Park* are primarily about the hidden sadness of plain women who do not expect to marry. In *Cranford*, Miss Jessie Brown and Miss Mattie Jenkyns are more or less compelled by family pressures to renounce marriage. Charlotte Yonge had discussed spinsters in *The Daisy Chain* and other novels. Charlotte Brontë had raged against their unfulfilled lives in *Shirley* and had left her heroine unmarried at the end of *Villette*. This was also the case in Margaret Oliphant's neglected classic, *Kirsteen* (1890).[54]

Flora Mayor had grown up on these novels but she (with an interesting contemporary, May Sinclair) was perhaps the first to write a clinical study of spinsterhood. There were various ways of explaining why a woman had failed in her prime task of catching a man. It could be argued that she was ugly or unfit for marriage, perhaps because her parents had stunted her emotional development. Or she might be an unselfish woman who had given up a lover for the sake of her family (like the aunt in *The Third Miss Symons*, or the heroine of May Sinclair's *Mary Olivier* [1919]). Or she could have had a lover who died; this had actually happened to Flora Mayor but, characteristically, she did not write about it.

It is clear that Henrietta Symons is not loved because she is not lovable, and she becomes even less lovable as her story goes on. The novel could be read as an awful warning to young women. Henrietta, with the same basic equipment as everyone else, will not try to please, rejects the good advice she gets about controlling her temper, and ends up a miserable unwanted spinster. But, of course, the moral is nothing like so simple. Flora Mayor did not believe that all spinsters were bitter and thwarted; her own unmarried aunts had led active and happy lives, and there are single women in the novel who have a much more positive outlook than Henrietta. They include her old teacher, Miss Arundel, and a number of other women she meets at the Greek lectures who 'used learning as a symbol of emancipation. Lectures were their vote. Now they would be in prison' (8). It takes us a moment to work out that Flora Mayor, writing around 1912, is referring to the militant suffragettes. Women can have multiple interests outside marriage; Henrietta has a good mind at the beginning of the story and there was no need for her to have let it decay. 'She is not so much wasted', wrote John Masefield in his Preface to the original edition, 'as not used.'

Yet women are not encouraged to use their minds in the
society which F. M. Mayor is depicting. Henrietta, born around
1850, is trained only for marriage and does not know what to
do with herself when this fails her. Novels (including *Jane Eyre*
and *Villette*, written by a frustrated spinster), give her 'a
completely erroneous view of life' (2). The years at home,
which were supposed to be 'a short period of preparation for
marriage', stretch out, leaving her with nothing to do. If her
parents had been poorer, 'she would have been forced to make
an effort; not to brood and concentrate herself on her misery',
but as things are she has to fall back on 'seven hours of
drawing-room fancy work' daily (4). She improves when she
takes on household responsibilities after her mother's death
but, again, novels and magazines have given her a false
impression that 'as the home daughter to a widowed father, the
home sister to two brothers, she would be consulted, leant on,
confided in' (6); this does not happen and no one regrets her
when she is displaced. After that she discovers 'the art of
getting through the day with the minimum of employment' (6).
Her activities become more and more trivial – reading bad
novels which she promptly forgets, playing patience, quarrelling,
abusing foreigners and servants. Examples of her conversation
are 'an endless story of a certain Elise who had stolen the
biscuits' (9), and 'tracing an attack of influenza from its source
to its decline' (12).

'What a piece of work is a man! How noble in reason, how
infinite in faculty . . . in action how like an angel, in
apprehension how like a god' (9). The author sardonically
quotes Shakespeare to illustrate the vast gap between what
Henrietta is and what she might have been. Up to a point, of
course, Henrietta is to blame, as are her family. But the real
culprit is the society which will not train girls for any career but
marriage (reflected in novels which teach women that the
family is their only source of happiness, when so many family
relationships are so far from perfect). It is not surprising that
Flora Mayor sympathised with the suffrage movement:

> Henry [her brother], while meaning to be perfectly fair-
> minded about women does really want to restrict them to the
> old-fashioned life which I think proved satisfactory when
> there was much more to be done in the household . . . but

now that is gone and can't come back and women must have
something more. And I do feel that looking round and
comparing old and the new, the new [women] are much
more livable with and wide-minded and less likely to take
offence.[55]

Yet emancipation is not the whole answer to the problems of
a Henrietta Symons. For her, unlike some women, 'the all-
sufficing condition of existence' is 'to love and be loved' (3). In
a passage which contains several layers of irony, we see that the
old schoolmistress, who seems so much more admirable than
Henrietta, may be her moral inferior:

> She might be something of a bore, but there was no question
> of her happiness, her interest in life. She had been getting up
> at six the last three mornings that she might finish a book, a
> large book in two volumes with close print, that had to be
> returned to the library. Henrietta could imagine nothing in
> the world for which she would get up at six o'clock. Then her
> thoughts went back like lightning to the morning when the
> telegram had come telling of little Madeline's death. The
> wound she had thought healed burst out afresh; for a few
> seconds she felt as if she could hardly breathe. Get up at six
> o'clock, of course she would have forfeited her sleep with joy,
> night after night. In the midst of envy, she felt something like
> contempt for Miss Arundel as a child running after shadows.
> (8)

It is ironic because Henrietta has never seen the sister's children
whom she loved so deeply; her relationships with the people she
actually knows are far less perfect. Yet her insight is a real one.
Coming from a family of scholars, F. M. Mayor was not likely
to undervalue the life of the intellect, but she also believed that
Miss Arundel (who had not given the desired response when
Henrietta wrote to her about learning Italian) has a less clear
vision that Henrietta of what life is about. With a desperate
longing for affection, Henrietta must be content with the
'crumbs which Evelyn can spare from her husband and children'
(13). She will put up with shameful treatment from men in
order to be liked, but men are not her sole interest; her only
real relationship is with her youngest sister. Nephews and

nieces are another outlet for affection but, as the author says rather bitingly, they 'were very much of the twentieth century, and were not going to bear with a dull old maid, merely because she was their aunt and had been kind to them' (10). With all her glaring faults, she does retain the basic virtues of generosity (constant money gifts to her family) and humility (the humility to stay away from other people when she knows she will be unable to get on with them). 'There was an impression in her mind', the author says, 'that as she had been out of it so much of her life she should be allowed to be bad-tempered as a consolation' (2); her faults are caused by her despair.

Evelyn's conventional remark, 'nothing in this life goes by deserts' (11) could be said to sum up this novel. Henrietta would have been a perfectly adequate wife for Mr Dockerell and is 'not uglier, or stupider, or duller than anyone else' (2). But superficial qualities – prettiness and apparent good temper – are more highly valued on the marriage market than the real, if modest, virtues Henrietta has got. The grumbling and nagging which turn people against her are actually far less unpleasant than Louie's dog-in-the-mangerish behaviour which, as Henrietta accurately says, spoils her life. Yet 'Louie was not merely let off scot-free for what she did, but was to have every happiness given to her. Why?' (3).

Clearly F. M. Mayor did not believe, like the older Victorians, that good and evil behaviour brought their own reward or punishment. (Indeed, in *The Rector's Daughter* she showed that the best women often have the hardest time.) She is very much a modern novelist in that respect, and also in the way she depicts the ebb and flow of emotion, particularly the meaner, less heroic kind. Thus, Henrietta forgets Mr Dockerell after a time, and resumes a fairly normal relationship with her married sisters, who sponge on her, but 'disliked being beholden to Henrietta, and, half intentionally, set their children against her to relieve their feelings' (6).

It may read like the chronicle of a wasted life, a story in which very few characters can be liked or respected. Flora Mayor was no more sentimental than Jane Austen (note the reference in Chapter 13 to a 'careful nephew' who takes his legacies as soon as Henrietta is dead). But the ending gives us a new perspective. We are startled out of the contempt which most of us would automatically feel for a Henrietta, and made to realise that, unlike her married sisters, she was able to give disinterested love: 'But if she had had the chance she wouldn't have been unlovable. She was capable of greater love than any of us, and she never had the chance' (13).

Evelyn asks 'if there is any justice and mercy in the world' when 'a poor, weak human creature' is allowed 'to have so few opportunities'. The answer seems to be that although the world is radically imperfect (which does not mean that it cannot be changed for the better), there is another world where 'the bitterness, aimlessness and emptiness of her life was made up to her' (13). Whether or not we believe this, the ending works because by this time most sensitive readers will feel a lot of sympathy for Henrietta. Several years later, F. M. Mayor wrote that many people, 'men and women, young and old' had admitted to her that they felt the Third Miss Symons was very like themselves – 'so I think that . . . all of us have a good deal of her in us'.[56]

The book demonstrated that every human being has a need to be loved and appreciated, that they can degenerate if these needs are not met, and that that most despised of figures, the old maid, has as much right to be taken seriously as anyone else. F. M. Mayor would explore another aspect of spinsterhood – devoted service to others – in *The Rector's Daughter*. But it is worth looking first at a novel which appeared between the two, *Life and Death of Harriett Frean* (1922). The author, May Sinclair (1863–1946) was, like Flora Mayor, unmarried and very interested in the problem of old maids. *Harriett Frean* may well have been influenced by *The Third Miss Symons*, as both are very short novels tracing the (outwardly) uneventful life of an English spinster from childhood until death. Both make it clear that the central figure has wasted her life, but in May Sinclair's book there is no redeeming glimpse at the end. She roundly blames Harriett's parents who have brought up their daughter to behave 'beautifully' whether or not this is appropriate. Like Maggie in *The Mill on the Floss* (a book which had an enormous influence on women novelists of this generation) Harriett refuses to marry a man who is engaged to another girl; as a result, all three are miserable. The cult of self-sacrifice, which all Victorian women had been taught, here comes under direct attack.

F. M. Mayor also believed that parents frequently damaged

their children; Mr and Mrs Symons certainly harm their daughter with their coldness and fault-finding, and Canon Jocelyn is an inadequate father. But she was less ready than May Sinclair to denounce the traditional Christian and womanly virtue of self-sacrifice, although she did not recommend it to all and sundry. *The Rector's Daughter* demonstrates that, in some circumstances, it can do good.

Like *The Third Miss Symons*, this is a novel about what is laughingly called an 'unnecessary female'. But while Henrietta is 'divorced from every duty, every responsibility, every natural tie' (9), Mary has almost too many duties for one person. Her adult life until the age of thirty-five has been spent looking after a handicapped sister; she keeps house for her father, who is basically indifferent to her, and she 'superintended the Sunday School, trained the Choir, had a boys' Bible Class and a Mothers' Meeting' (2). Her last years are spent looking after an irritating aunt and we are told that 'her solace, sometimes severe, were the duties that sprang up in the little home' (27) – duties like winding the clock, letting the cat out, listening to Aunt Lottie's dreary gossip, overseeing the knitting – and so on for the rest of her life.

'Duties' – there could hardly be a more typically Victorian word, and the author was quite aware that many readers would react to it with irritation and boredom. But Mary's problem is that she is neither 'Victorian' nor 'modern'; the book, set in the early years of the twentieth century, shows her living with her octogenarian father in a home which is 'a frail, frail survival, lasting on out of its time, its companions vanished long since, and would fall at a touch when Canon Jocelyn died' (1). She is ill at ease with her own generation and reads Trollope and Miss Yonge, not contemporary authors. Yet she shares Mr Herbert's sense that their generation has lost the 'abounding, buoyant faith' of their parents (13). Much of the novel is a thoughtful weighing-up of the weaknesses and strengths of old and new.

Like most great novels, it has its distinctive atmosphere. Mary lives in the East Anglian village of Dedmayne (the pun is intentional), 'mouldering along', as she says, 'year after year' (1). It appears fairly ugly with its 'low dusty hedges' and 'treeless turnip fields', yet it also has the great winds which represent passion, and its mud, insignificant wild flowers, toads and so on, are more appealing to Mary than the conventional prettiness of the suburb where she eventually dies. Naturally, the centre of village life is the church, with its musty smell and its fine old prayer books which Kathy's friends deface. Mary likes going because among other things it makes her feel closer to the Dedmayne people 'gone from the earth over a hundred years ago' (11). This is the positive side of the Church; the other is the Clerical Book Club Tea and various boring activities which Mary has to organise because no one else will. Then there is the Rectory which overflows with books, especially Bibles and the classics (compare Brynhilda's flat where none of the books are more than a few years old), but which is pervaded with 'a crumbling decay', has a pond like a 'monster slug', and is 'as dark as a vault' because of the evergreens growing outside (1).

Mary is living at the end of a great tradition of religion and scholarship – listening to the Canon talk is like reading good Victorian prose – yet her home is emphatically a place of darkness and decay. The Canon values his sons above his daughters and takes no real interest in any of his children: 'he became occupied with St Augustine, and had no leisure for her' (2). As he realises himself (26), his Christianity is of the brain and not the heart; his approach to child-rearing is 'disastrous' (13); some of his prejudices are absurd. When he mentions George Eliot (his own contemporary) and says that 'to indulge in love for a married man is always illicit' (16) Mary realises that there is a great gulf between them; he can never be expected to understand her own illicit love for Mr Herbert.

The novel, as a critic said, 'is like a bitter *Cranford*'.[57] Mary in her backwater sees only one man she can love, 'with real love, not a sort of heavenly thing up in the sky' (29). She loses him to a younger and more attractive woman; it is just one of life's ironies that Kathy could have married several other men while this is Mary's sole chance. Very few things ever *happen* to her (whereas Kathy has quite a few adventures); she can only wait while Mr Herbert vacillates and, as in *Persuasion* and some Brontë novels, the whole focus is on the drama of her inner life. And she cannot accept her fate as sweetly as the ladies of *Cranford*. Cursed with more intense feelings than most people, she undergoes the pain of extreme guilt, desire and frustration, and feels for a time that she is 'outcast from God' (16). Her

attempts to tell her father and her unimaginative friend Dora
are balked because she knows they would both feel that she is a
sinner.

It is, of course, this crisis which shows up the gap between
'old' and 'new' moralities most sharply. Yet Mary does not get
much more comfort from Brynhilda's set, who were, apparently,
based on Virginia Woolf and her pre-war circle. London, 'with
its taxis scarlet and emerald, and its buses like dressed-up
revellers at a ball' (11), is obviously, a thrilling place compared to
Dedmayne. 'There is a particular charm in those damp London
twilights', the author notes, 'a freedom from the weight of
routine, responsibility, and duty, which suited well with Mary's
present thoughts' (11). But she and Brynhilda's group turn out to
be incompatible. The latter form 'light elastic unions'; they are
repelled by strong feelings; they include a girl called Priscilla
who sees sex as a series of 'adventures' which 'go on and on
and on' (11). 'It was strange to think Dora and she belonged to
the same nation', Mary reflects (13). She knows they would
encourage her to have a full-blooded affair with Mr Herbert on
the grounds that 'life is meant for experience' (11): 'She could
imagine with what pleasant, easy principles of guidance
Brynhilda would have supported her inclination. She shrank
from that too' (16).

'She had a life so shrivelled it became absurd', Brynhilda
sums up. 'She ought to have been married to that man and
been happy. People one knows marry, and divorce, and have
children, and are bored the whole time. How crazy it all is, and
how tragic' (28).

The author felt little affinity with these bright young people
(who belong at least as much to the 1920s as to the period of
the novel) and made no attempt to get inside their skins. On
the other hand, she did make a real effort to understand the
philistine Kathy, who was not at all her own type. Since it is
Mary's story, and we are likely to feel a good deal of sympathy
with her, we do not expect to have much time for Kathy, and it
is a real achievement on Flora Mayor's part to make us see
things from her point of view. There is a clash of cultures in the
Herbert marriage just as there is in the wider world. Mr
Herbert and his mother, who are basically the same sort of
people as Canon Jocelyn and Mary, have their teeth set on

edge by her 'flighty exterior', her cigarettes and bridge-playing, her indifference to the things of the mind:

> Their forebears had been statesmen and bishops, distinguished in learning and courtliness. The contempt which the rustic, uncultivated county had for such as the Herberts they heartily returned. Neither side realised that both alike were doomed, their one hope a combination against the 'new rich'.   (15)

This is a tantalising hint, which is not fully developed. But we may assume that the 'new rich' are the people with whom Kathy spends a winter in Monte Carlo, a group for whom the author had no more respect than she had for the London literati. Kathy herself soon gets tired of them and wants 'to be back at her regular duties – feeding the fowls, ordering the dinner, teaching the village boys woodwork' (16). (Note that word 'duties' again.) She misses 'twilight falling over the English fields' (19), although she cannot put this into words. 'She was not one of those who demand everything that life can offer. She was perfectly happy leading a jog-trot existence in the country with two dogs, a horse, and her husband' (15).

It is implied here that the English countryside, dull as it may seem, does after all provide the basis for a meaningful life. The marriage eventually turns out well; Mr Herbert realises that 'living in the twentieth century, and having definitely joined the party of the younger generation, it was no good wincing at what he formerly had considered vulgarity' (24). He does not expect his wife to be his intellectual equal (retreating to his Cambridge college when he wants good conversation), but he does not consider her a mere housekeeper or sex object either. He, Mary and the reader all have to learn that Kathy is neither an 'all-conquering beauty' (15) nor a boring impediment, but a basically decent and vulnerable human being.

It is hardest for Mary, of course. When Kathy is in the Riviera and Herbert appears to love and need her she barely manages to resist temptation. Not that it is ever really possible that they should run away together, being who they are and living where they do. 'Mary knew no mercy would be felt for a middle-aged married clergyman who had been disloyal to his wife; less than none for a middle-aged spinster' (16). The real

struggle has to be fought out within her mind, the struggle not
to be 'thinking of pleasure she was ashamed to own':

> She would picture Kathy's death. After a while she went
> further and pictured her going away with another man, Mr
> Herbert's freedom, and their marriage. If she had been told a
> month ago she would have desired the death, still more the
> sin of another woman, she would not have believed it. . . .
> The spirit of the times was making itself felt in her.   (16)

There are other suggestions in Flora Mayor's work and letters
that civilisation was changing for the worse. We may doubt
whether Mary's daydreams are really 'the spirit of the times' or
the basic human weakness of wanting inconvenient people out
of the way. But she is letting herself hope that, as in countless
romantic novels, including *Jane Eyre*, her rival will be removed
by an act of God – and she is never comfortable with this. In
the end, she comes to like and respect Kathy, helps her through
her worst time, and sees that she was right not to have
interfered in the Herberts' marriage. 'It was to the plain,
middle-aged woman she owed her restored happiness', Kathy
acknowledges at the end of the novel (29).

It is Mary's fate to be always looking after the people no one
else wants, like her sister and Canon Jocelyn (other people
think she is glad to be rid of them, but she is not). Then there
are the solitary middle-aged women like herself: Aunt Lottie
whom she goes to live with because 'Aunt Lottie could turn to
no one else' (26), and Mrs Plumtree and Miss Davey with
whom she has to endure 'six hours of chat' (17) every night.
This kind of life may be easy for a family of unmarried 'girls'
like the Redlands, who have never wanted anything else and
who have 'the wonderful desire which is so strong in English
spinsters to serve, to help, to be perhaps almost too busy in
other people's affairs' (18). For Mary, who does want something
more, it is tempting to sink into a Henrietta Symons:

> In youth she had resolved not to yield to the luxury of self-
> pity. That resolution had not been kept . . . . The recollection
> frightened her. She had found self-pity a quagmire in which
> it was difficult not to be submerged.   (27)

'I feel very much the sadness of Mary's wasted powers –', Flora had written. Mary Jocelyn's life is wasted in all the obvious ways; her poems, which seem to have had some value, are lost; the one man who cares for her nevertheless marries someone else; she does not get the children she wants. Even a meaningful parting from Mr Herbert is denied her and she last sees him at a matinée (this kind of realism is characteristic of the author). There is a strong suggestion that she dies from an ordinary attack of 'flu because she lacks the will to live. Only her self-respect and, eventually, her religion sustain her:

Going on with her outer life she had from henceforth an inner life, and whereas her circle was cheerfully absorbed in the present, she thought much of the past and of the future, feeling the truth of words, which most people find disturbing. 'We have here no continuing city; we seek that which is to come.' (27)

As even Dora says, 'How glad one is . . . that this life isn't all' (8). If it were, it is implied, the profound unfairness would be too much to bear.

Flora Mayor's subject-matter – the lives and experiences of English spinsters – seems limited. Yet English spinsters have written some of our finest novels, and she is a much better writer than others in the same tradition, such as Charlotte Yonge, who got more fame in their day. Perhaps we tend to write her off because we assume that women – particularly unattached, unwanted women – are not important. Her work should make us re-examine that belief.

4

Katherine Mansfield

From the other side of the world,
From a little island cradled in the giant sea bosom,
From a little land with no history,
(Making its own history, slowly and clumsily
Piecing together this and that, finding the pattern,
   solving the problem,
Like a child with a box of bricks),
I, a woman, with the taint of the pioneer in my blood,
Full of a youthful strength that wars with itself and
   is lawless . . . .[58]

So Katherine Mansfield, aged twenty-one and happy to have escaped to Europe, described herself. Several years later and nearing the end of her short life, she wrote, 'The longer I live the more I turn to New Zealand. I thank God I was born in New Zealand. A young country is a real heritage, though it takes one time to recognise it. But New Zealand is in my very bones.'[59]

The country had become British in 1840, since when it had received a flood of emigrants from the Old World. They were mainly hard-working people with few intellectual interests. 'We will all agree . . . that a national literature has not yet been created here',[60] wrote an anthologist in 1883. The most famous of all New Zealand writers was born five years later, in Wellington on 14 October 1888, and named Kathleen Mansfield Beauchamp.

Her father, Harold, was a successful self-made businessman (later Chairman of the Bank of New Zealand), whose own father, the son of a London silversmith, had come to the Antipodes in 1848. He had hoped for a boy (who was not born until 1894), so Kathleen, the third daughter, was probably not

particularly welcome. Her mother, formerly Annie Dyer, seems
to have been a singularly cold woman. It was her grandmother
who was the real parent-figure.

In 1893 Harold Beauchamp moved his family out of town to
the little settlement of Karori (the setting of 'Prelude'), where
they lived for the next five years and where Kathleen went to
school. A fat, plain, rather surly child who read and wrote
incessantly, she was already very much the odd one out. After
the Beauchamps had moved back to Wellington she and her
sisters were educated at some expensive girls' schools and
then, in 1903, went to England to study at Queen's College,
London.

Kathleen was overwhelmed by Europe. She considered
becoming a professional cello player, and tried to model herself
on Oscar Wilde and the 'decadent' poets. For her generation,
her husband wrote, 'the decadents were the gateway to the
imaginative life'.[61] When her parents took her back to New
Zealand, three years later, she resolved to 'make myself so
objectionable that they'll *have* to send me away'.[62] A note in her
journal for 1907 reads: 'Damn my family! O Heavens, what
bores they are! I detest them all heartily. I shall certainly not
be here much longer. Thank Heaven for that!'[63] She had no
wish to go to parties or to catch a suitable husband. 'We are all
sent into the world to develop ourselves to the very fullest
extent . . . and here there is really no scope for development –
no intellectual society – no hope of finding any',[64] she wrote.
Self-consciously, she described herself as 'seized by a passionate
desire for everything that is hidden and forbidden'.[65] Some 'sex-
problem' stories which she wrote in New Zealand struck a
reader as the work of 'a matured and widely experienced
woman of thirty'.[66] At last, after long and bitter arguments with
her parents, she got their permission to live in London on an
allowance, and sailed in July 1908. She was not quite twenty,
and would never see New Zealand again.

We know little about her life during the next three years. She
had turned into a strikingly attractive young woman with an
enigmatic personality; friends commented on her 'chameleon
quality'[67] and habit of keeping her life in separate compartments.
Her husband said later that she 'belonged, by birthright, to the
"experiencing natures"'.[68] Both before and after leaving home,

she had several affairs. Even today Kathleen's behaviour at this
stage of her life would seem promiscuous; for a gently-bred girl
in the 1900s, it was outrageous.

Some of this 'experience', she thought afterwards, had been
destructive.[69] Just after reaching London she became involved
with a young musician from New Zealand, Garnet Trowell.
There was a quarrel and, on 2 March 1909, she suddenly
married George Bowden, a singer. She left him the same day
and returned to Trowell, but the relationship broke up just
after she had become pregnant. Her mother arrived from New
Zealand, took her to a Bavarian spa, and left her there.
Kathleen had a miscarriage a few weeks later. She returned to
London and, in 1910, was ill with 'rheumatic fever'. It was
really a form of venereal disease and this, apparently, made it
impossible for her to have any more children.

Around this time she began to publish short pieces in the
radical weekly *The New Age*, under the name of Katherine
Mansfield. Some of them were sketches of her life in Bavaria,
afterwards collected in a book, *In a German Pension* (1911). It
was well received, but she decided later that it had been
worthless. Towards the end of 1910 she visited the post-
Impressionist exhibition which, according to Virginia Woolf,
changed human nature. Years later, Katherine described the
effect of Van Gogh's sunflower painting:

> That picture seemed to reveal something that I hadn't
> realised before I saw it. It lived with me afterwards. It still
> does. That and another of a sea-captain in a flat cap. They
> taught me something about writing, which was queer, a kind
> of freedom – or rather, a shaking free.[70]

She had already decided to shake herself free from the
traditional novel, which so many hopeful young men and
women were writing; her chosen form was the short story. She
is often said to have been influenced by Chekhov and later she
certainly admired him tremendously, but at the time she had
not read much of his work. It was to be some years before she
wrote anything especially valuable or characteristic. At the end
of 1911 she sent a New Zealand story, 'The Woman at the
Store', to a small magazine, *Rhythm*. The young editor, John

Middleton Murry, was impressed. They met and quickly fell in love.

Murry, who came from a fairly poor background, had won a scholarship to Oxford and was still officially an undergraduate when Katherine met him. He had decided that he wanted to write rather than have a conventional career, and he was to become one of the best known, though not one of the most respected, literary critics of his generation. Their relationship, which lasted until Katherine's death, had its bad patches, and the two often lived apart for months, by choice or necessity. Afterwards Murry liked to quote from one of her last letters, 'in spite of all, no truer lovers ever walked the earth than we were'.[71] But they were an odd and unconventional couple. He never paid Katherine's bills, even after they were married, and he often failed to give her much-needed emotional support.

In 1912 Murry moved into her flat and she became the assistant editor of *Rhythm*. It quickly sank, like so many little magazines, and had a short-lived successor, *The Blue Review*. Through their work they met D. H. Lawrence and were present at his marriage to Frieda a month before the beginning of the war.

Murry was excused from military service on health grounds and they continued to live, very cheaply, on her allowance and their small literary earnings. Neither of them wanted to be involved with the war effort and over the next few years they became friendly with the Garsington set which included such anti-war activists as Bertrand Russell. Katherine visited the war zone early in 1915 to see her then lover, the novelist Francis Carco. (This was to be a mere hiccup in her relationship with Murry.) Her story, 'An Indiscreet Journey', was the result. Later in the year she made other visits to the non-combatant sector of France to write.

But although she tried to behave as if the war was not happening, it brought her a searing emotional and artistic experience. In 1915 her young brother, Leslie Beauchamp, had come to England to join up. He was the only boy and the hope of the family. Katherine saw a good deal of him and began to write *The Aloe* after he had revived her memories of New Zealand. In October Leslie was accidentally killed in France by a hand grenade. *The Aloe*, revised and published as 'Prelude', became a kind of elegy for their childhood.

In 1916 she and Murry took a cottage in Cornwall near the Lawrences. It was not a success. She detested Frieda, liked Lawrence (and was one of the first to recognise his genius), but wrote privately, 'I shall *never* see sex in trees, sex in the running brooks, sex in stones and sex in everything'.[72] Lawrence greatly resented her influence over Murry. He was writing *Women in Love* at this time and put them into it as Gudrun and Gerald. The chapter 'Gudrun in the Pompadour' was based on a real incident when Katherine had snatched a book of Lawrence's poems from some strangers who were making fun of them.

Murry obtained work in military intelligence later in the year (the alternative would have been doing unskilled work for the army). Katherine moved with him to Bloomsbury and met Leonard and Virginia Woolf, who published her long story 'Prelude' on the Hogarth Press in 1918. But before that, around Christmas 1917, a doctor had examined her and found a spot on one lung.

For the rest of her life (exactly five years) she knew that she was mortally ill. She had written only a fraction of her best work; now it became a race against time. She spent the beginning of 1918 in the South of France, nursed by her devoted friend Ida Baker and writing 'Je ne parle pas français' and 'Bliss'. But conditions were much worse than at the beginning of the war, and her health declined rapidly. On the way back she was trapped for three weeks in Paris while it was being bombed. When she returned to England her divorce from George Bowden came through and she and Murry were married on 3 May. Specialists who examined her advised her to enter a sanatorium – saying, accurately, that she could expect to live for four years if she did not – but she refused, probably because it would have interfered with her work.

Released from the War Office by the Armistice, Murry was appointed editor of the *Athenaeum* with a large salary. Katherine reviewed novels for the magazine and saw a good deal of T. S. Eliot and Virginia Woolf. But she could no longer spend the winters in England, and went for long periods to the Continent where several of her best stories were written. A volume, *Bliss and Other Stories* (which contained earlier and weaker work) was published in 1920 and got enthusiastic reviews.

She was now spitting blood and unable to walk more than a few yards. Her loneliness was intense as Murry was kept in

London by his work and, anyway, was not the man to cope
with an invalid wife. He was grudging about money and
rumours reached her of his relationships with other women. In
1919 she wrote:

> It isn't a married life at all – not what I mean by a married
> life. How I envy Virginia; no wonder she can write. There is
> always in her writing a calm freedom of expression as though
> she were at peace – her roof over her, her possessions round
> her, and her man somewhere within call.[73]

At another time she said that Murry ought to divorce her and
marry someone in normal health. Yet, as a later letter to him
shows, she did eventually come to terms with what was
happening:

> *Everything has its shadow.* Is it right to resist such suffering? Do
> you know I feel it has been an immense privilege. Yes, in
> spite of all . . . if someone rebels and says, Life isn't good
> enough on those terms, one can only say: 'It *is!'* . . . . We
> resist, we are terribly frightened. The little boat enters the
> dark fearful gulf and our only cry is to escape – 'put me on
> land again'. But it's useless. Nobody listens. The shadowy
> figure rows on. One ought to sit still and uncover one's
> eyes.[74]

When this was written, in October 1920, she was about to
write some outstanding stories – 'The Stranger', 'Miss Brill',
'The Daughters of the Late Colonel'. Other stories with a New
Zealand setting – 'At the Bay', 'The Garden Party', 'The Doll's
House' – were written in Switzerland in 1921. Unfortunately,
there was never quite enough money to pay her medical bills,
and for this reason she felt compelled to write and sell stories
('Mr and Mrs Dove') which she knew to be inferior.

Her best collection, *The Garden Party and Other Stories*, came
out in February 1922. There were a few more mature stories,
including 'The Fly'. But by the late summer she had stopped
writing – according to Murry, not because of physical weakness
but because 'she felt that her whole attitude to life needed to be
renewed, and she determined that she would write no more
until it had been renewed.'[75] Having failed to find a conventional

cure, she had come under the influence of a Greek, George Ivanovich Gurdjieff, who had started a community near Fontainebleau to promote 'harmonious development'. She lived there happily for three months, sometimes doing light work in the kitchen. In her last letter she wrote, 'I want much more material; I am tired of my little stories like birds bred in cages'.[76] On 9 January 1923 Murry arrived for a visit, but Katherine had a haemorrhage the same evening and died.

'I was jealous of her writing', Virginia Woolf confided to her diary, '– the only writing I have ever been jealous of.'[77]

Thirty years later F. R. Leavis complained of 'how the tiny talent of Katherine Mansfield was acclaimed: how promptly, and to what an inflationary tune'.[78] Murry, who remained obsessed with her until his death in 1957, published nearly all her work – letters, journals, unfinished stories – and did not hesitate to call her a genius of the same quality as Blake and Keats. Because she had been close to the centre of the literary establishment at a time when literary values were changing drastically, her reputation was never allowed to decline. Short stories are supposed to be difficult to sell, but her work has never gone out of print and has been widely translated; streets and poems have been dedicated to her, and she became a legend within a very few years of her death.

Interestingly enough, Murry also used the word 'tiny' to describe her work – 'In scope Katherine Mansfield was a tiny artist; but because she was a pure artist, she was a great one.'[79] Her biographers talk about 'her love for little tiny things – exquisite, minute flowers and shells'.[80] In 'Prelude' the Katherine-figure, Kezia, has a habit of making matchbox pictures:

> First she would put a leaf inside with a big violet lying on it, then she would put a very small white picotee, perhaps, on each side of the violet, and then she would sprinkle some lavender on the top, but not to cover their heads. (6)

Her stories, artefacts themselves, are full of other artefacts; the cake in 'Sun and Moon', the enamel box in 'A Cup of Tea' (not *just* a rich woman's toy), the doll's house and particularly its little lamp. The need to make small, perfect things may have been rooted in imaginative child's play as described in 'Prelude':

> In front of each person she put two geranium leaf plates, a
> pine needle fork and a twig knife. There were three daisy
> heads on a laurel leaf for poached eggs, some slices of fuchsia
> petal cold beef, some lovely little rissoles made of earth and
> water and dandelion seeds, and the chocolate custard.   (8)

At this point the children are called and leave the 'charming
table' 'to the ants and to an old snail who . . . began to nibble
at a geranium plate'. (A whole story is built on a similar event
in 'Sun and Moon'.) Katherine Mansfield was haunted by the
image of 'the snail beneath the leaf', which symbolised
destruction. In a famous letter of 1918, she said that her work
was motivated by the wish to express 'something delicate and
lovely', but also by 'an *extremely* deep sense of hopelessness, of
everything doomed to disaster, almost wilfully, stupidly', and
was therefore 'a cry against corruption'.[81] Themes of making
and spoiling dominate her work.

She was a woman who had deliberately ventured out of a
sheltered background (when she stays inside it, her stories are
fairly trivial) and exposed herself to various forms of cruelty
and isolation. The woman in 'Revelations' tells herself: 'It is
the loneliness which is so appalling. We whirl along like leaves,
and nobody knows – nobody cares where we fall, in what black
river we float away.' Her usual method is to show the
'loneliness', or horror, gradually breaking into the awareness of
a central character, who is usually a woman from a background
like her own or a very young child. However, the two best of
her early stories, 'The Woman at the Store' and 'Millie', are
untypical. They are both New Zealand stories, set in he wilder
part of the country where she had travelled as a nineteen-year-
old girl, which confront violence directly. The heroines, if that
is the right word, are unromanticised; pioneer women who use
guns; the woman at the store has murdered her husband
because he has 'broken her spirit and spoiled her looks' by
forcing her to live in the bush. Millie feels that men 'is all
beasts', and, in the horrifying climax, enjoys watching one of
them hunted down. The atmosphere is one of heat, flies, and a
primitive level of culture. Millie has a print of a garden party at

Windsor Castle, whose 'emerald lawns', 'oak trees, and in their grateful shade a muddle of ladies and gentlemen and parasols and little tables' contrast cruelly with her own situation. Katherine Mansfield came back to the garden party theme several years later, but then it was to show the rich gazing voyeuristically at the poor instead of the other way round. They are powerful stories, but she was probably wise to write no more of them; even if she had stayed in New Zealand, the experiences of such people would still have been too remote from her own.

The same resentment against men appears in her German stories, notably 'Frau Brechenmacher Attends a Wedding'. And, in several stories written over the next seven years, she shows women being exploited – but, it should be noted, without offering them much sympathy.

'The Little Governess' is one of the best of these stories, although its effect is such that few will want to read it a second time. Governesses are archetypal figures in the English novel, vulnerable young women from middle-class backgrounds who are forced out into a harsh world. This particular young woman is travelling alone, at night, and in a 'cold, strange wind' (the wind is always a significant image for Katherine Mansfield). She ends up in a foreign country with her job, as well as her illusions, lost. There almost seems to be a male conspiracy against her, from the porter who tears off the 'Dames Seules' label, to the waiter, the men in the next carriage and of course the unpleasant old German. But the author appears to share the bystanders' mocking attitude. The first sentence, 'Oh, dear, how she wished that it wasn't night-time' suggests that she has an immature personality; there are hints, too, that she behaves arrogantly by snubbing the porter and waiter and so makes things worse for herself. And the sugary description of her means the opposite of what it appears to mean:

> Alas! how tragic for a little governess to possess hair that made one think of tangerines and marigolds, of apricots and tortoiseshell cats and champagne! Perhaps that was what the old man was thinking as he gazed and gazed .... Perhaps the flush that licked his cheeks and lips was a flush of rage that anyone so young and tender should have to travel alone and unprotected through the night.

But we find out, if we have not already guessed, that the old man was really thinking nothing of the sort. The governess, like Beryl in the New Zealand stories, is weaving fantasies about herself and her effect on men. Nourished on these fantasies like so many women, she happily accepts him as a grandfather, 'just like one out of a book', until he reveals what he is really after: 'It was a dream! It wasn't true! It wasn't the same old man at all.' The mocking note is unmistakable.

If there is a moral, it seems to be that women should grow up quickly and accept the world on its own terms. This appears to be the point of 'Pictures', whose heroine cannot possibly be seen in romantic terms. Miss Ada Moss is a middle-aged actress and singer who cannot get the jobs she needs to pay her rent. In a later story, 'Miss Brill', Katherine Mansfield treated the older, unwanted woman with compassion, but there is none here. The atmosphere is hard, cold and trivialising; the war (it was written in 1917) appears only in references to brooches from Dieppe or 'my poor dear lad in France'. Miss Moss is deliberately made an unlovely figure. Her room stinks of fried potatoes; she has an 'old dead powder-puff'; her legs are fat with 'great knots of greeny-blue veins'. The author had begun to take a deep interest in the fantasy life, and Miss Moss's daydreams have an independent life of their own. 'A pageant of Good Hot Dinners passed across the ceiling' on the first page; near the end she visualises a 'dark handsome gentleman' who is looking for a contralto. But of course she has no way out but prostitution, and her final decision to let herself be picked up is described in a cheerful matter-of-fact tone.

Equally unkind is the famous story 'Bliss'. Bertha Young at thirty is still 'young' at heart because she feels extreme happiness for no obvious reason. This could be seen as a good quality, but is not in Bertha because she is too obviously a woman who has no real understanding of her husband and child (the husband is uninterested in the child too, for that matter) and imagines she has a special relationship with Pearl Fulton, who is deceiving her. The radiant blossoming pear tree seems to her 'a symbol of her own life'. If it is, we can assume that there are snails beneath the leaves.

The story centres on a meal and critics have pointed out that it is full of food-imagery – luxurious food such as lobsters, cream and pistachio ices. We cannot be sure, in the scene where Bertha plays with the fruit, whether she is genuinely responding to its beauty or whether buying purple grapes to match the carpet is not the whim of a person with nothing more urgent to do. But Harry's remark, 'We only have a new coffee machine once a fortnight' does suggest strongly that the Youngs are nothing but consumers (using the word in its modern as well as its old-fashioned sense). The dinner-guests are trivial, falsely-clever people (like the guests in 'Marriage à la Mode', where it is the husband who is exploited). Katherine Mansfield's sympathy for the decadent movement had quite gone by 1918. She shows us a corrupt world, exposed for what it is by Harry's secret affair with Pearl Fulton, no pure romance this as we may judge from his 'hideous grin'. But, as in 'The Little Governess', our final impression is that the victim is too stupid to be pitied: 'Bertha simply ran over to the long windows. "Oh, what is going to happen now?" she cried.' The childish language mirrors her undeveloped mind.

It will be clear from all this that Katherine Mansfield had a distinct vein of cruelty, and she developed this in the long story 'Je ne parle pas français', which is a study of a 'superficial and impudent and cheap' sensibility. Again, in this story, the girl is abandoned by men who are weak or spiteful or both. But, as she said, the 'cry against corruption' was only one aspect of her work. After her brother's death she began to long to recreate the simpler life of their childhood. 'If the truth were known', she wrote in 1917, 'I have a perfect passion for the island where I was born . . . . I always remember feeling that this little island has dipped back into the dark blue sea during the night only to rise again at gleam of day, all hung with bright spangles and glittering drops . . . . I tried to lift that mist from my people and let them be seen.'[82] 'Prelude' and its sequel 'At the Bay' (which was written five years later, but may as well be studied in the same place) grew from her impulse to rescue something which, she now felt, was deeply meaningful.

'Prelude' was hardly the kind of story its readers expected. Bertrand Russell, in prison for anti-war activities, thought it 'trivial and worthless – it was bad enough that such trivial things should happen, without having to read descriptions of them'.[83] Certainly these two long stories, with their pictures of a few days in the lives of an ordinary family, could easily appear trivial, especially during and just after the war. But it was precisely because of the war, and what it had done to the human psyche, that Katherine Mansfield felt the traditional novel was played out. After reading Virginia Woolf's unsatisfactory early work, *Night and Day*, she wrote:

> the novel can't just leave the war out. There *must* have been a change of heart . . . . I feel in the *profoundest* sense that nothing can ever be the same – that, as artists, we are traitors if we feel otherwise: we have to take it into account and find new expressions, new moulds for our new thoughts and feelings. Is this exaggeration? What *has* been, stands, but Jane Austen could not write *Northanger Abbey* now – or if she did, I'd have none of her.[84]

This did not mean that artists should necessarily write *about* the war, which she knew that she was not qualified to do. 'It's not in the least a question of material or style or plot', she wrote around the same time. 'I can only think in terms like "a change of heart".'[85] For her, this meant resisting pressures to write what her editors called 'a nice "plotty" story'[86] and following her instincts. She wanted to celebrate Leslie, and her dead grandmother, and a childhood before the turn of the century. 'Plot' in the conventional sense would only have got in her way.

In these stories, set around the time the Beauchamp family moved out of Wellington to Karori, Katherine Mansfield introduced several real people – her parents and grandmother, Pat the handyman, the deprived Kelvey children in 'The Doll's House'. She herself appears as the child Kezia who is that much more sensitive and aware than her sisters, although Kezia is not the central figure. Understandably, people in New Zealand thought 'what she had done was very easy to do; it consisted in "copying" the characters she had known'.[87] But if we compare 'Prelude' to the much longer *The Aloe* from which it was quarried, we can see that she took enormous pains to improve the text and to cut out irrelevant material. The finished stories should be read in the same way as poetry; there can be no rushing through the descriptive passages to see what happens next. But one thing they do have in common with the traditional novel is their penetrating studies of character.

'Nothing happens', the reader may complain. The events are

extremely simple: a move to the country, night following day, the birth of a baby off-stage. Yet the essence of the Burnell family's situation is that nothing will happen. Linda dreams of getting away, Beryl fantasises about a lover, but neither of these things is possible. They will go on servicing the man of the house and, in Linda's case, bearing his children. Although Katherine Mansfield had been unattracted by what she saw of the suffragette movement, there is a great deal of subdued feminism in these stories.

When Stanley is at home, everything centres around his needs; he is constantly making the women and children run errands for him and they are relieved when he goes. Stanley is by no means a bad man. But he is totally dominated by the values of the market-place; the house, in the primeval bush, impresses him merely as a good investment and the sea is a goal he wants to reach before the other men 'There was something pathetic in his determination to make a job of everything', reflects his polar opposite, Jonathan ('At the Bay', 2). But Jonathan, who dislikes the commercial system but will never break free of it, is a pathetic figure too. He is perceptive enough to see that there is a 'vast dangerous garden . . . undiscovered, unexplored' outside the little world which Stanley inhabits, but he is 'like an insect' trapped among office furniture ('At the Bay', 10) – an image that would reappear in the author's most famous story.

Trapped, too, is Linda, aware that Stanley is a good husband yet hating him because he has chained her to her biological function. It is not clear whether she is to go on having children indefinitely or until she gets a son, but 'the boy' is extremely important to Stanley as the heir to the business. Linda shows her resentment by opting out of family life and refusing to care for her children, so there is nothing left for her to do. She is aware of the small flowers which represent value and meaning, but has no 'time to know them'. 'As soon as one paused to part the petals, to discover the under-side of the leaf, along came Life and one was swept away . . . . She was seized and shaken; she had to go. Oh dear, would it always be so? Was there no escape?' ('At the Bay', 6).

Not for her, evidently. Nor does there seem to be any escape for Beryl, like her sister an unmaternal type but coveting the married state which Linda finds oppressive. For her the move to the country means that she will 'rot' ('Prelude', 6) in a place without eligible men. As she realises at the end of 'Prelude', she has a real and a false self; the false one who is the heroine of a romantic novel and the real one, less easy to define, who must be satisfied by brief and degrading encounters with men.

Very different from both these women is their mother, Mrs Fairfield, who is the only real mother to Kezia. She is very definitely a traditional woman, getting her deepest satisfactions from running the household. We see her presiding over the table with her hand on a loaf of bread: 'Everything on the table flashed and glittered. In the middle there was an old salad bowl filled with yellow and red nasturtiums. She smiled, and a look of deep content shone in her eyes' ('At the Bay', 3). She has accepted the death of her son, since she has no choice, and that is part of her strength. When we last hear of her, 'the quick dark' is 'racing over the sea, over the sand-hills, up the paddock', but the grandmother is making sense of it by lighting a lamp.

Rituals like the lamp-lighting and setting of the table are necessary because outside the family circle lurk dangers – the 'tall dark trees and strange bushes' ('Prelude', 6), the hot sun, the sea. Linda is afraid of Stanley because he 'rushes at her' (this is a metapor, of course), and Kezia dreams of animals that rush at *her* ('Prelude', 3). Then there is the killing of the white duck; for Stanley it is merely 'the first of the home products' ('Prelude', 11), but for Kezia this is her first contact with violence. In 'At the Bay' the sun can kill and more violence is concealed underwater. 'There was a glimpse of a black feeler . . . a thread-like creature wavered by and was lost . . . . Who made that sound? What was going on down there?' (7).

The children are only marginally aware of violence; not at all aware of the tensions between the adults or Stanley's business world; the 'lovely green thing' which they find really is an emerald for them ('At the Bay', 4). The baby does not believe in his mother's indifference and Kezia does not believe she will die. In a sense, they are right. 'At the Bay' moves towards its close with a frightening face at the window, and darkness coming down. But at the very end, just after the ugly little episode between Beryl and Harry Kember, 'a cloud, small, serene, floated across the moon . . . all was still'.

Katherine's biographer has suggested that 'At the Bay' was

written as a response to Lawrence's *Women in Love*, which had
just been published, and to celebrate family love.[88] She did not
do this by pretending there were no conflicts within families.
But 'Prelude' and 'At the Bay' genuinely are an act of
celebration. Her family (once despised) are set for ever in the
context of New Zealand's land- and seascape, the once-in-a-
hundred-year-flowering aloe, the rhythms of day and night. 'I
efface myself', Katherine wrote, 'so that you may live again
through me in your richness and beauty.'[89]

In 'Daughters of the Late Colonel', one of the longest and most
impressive of her stories, the method is similar to that of
'Prelude' and 'At the Bay'. She is not concerned to show things
happening, when nothing is likely ever to happen to Josephine
and Constantia; instead she concentrates on the apparently
trivial in order to show us the reality of their inner lives. With
the same subject-matter as Flora Mayor, she employs a quite
different technique. We are not told until the end that the
sisters might have married if their father had been another kind
of man; instead we are taken directly into their fantasy life.
    It is a rich and overflowing one. They daydream about the
porter's head, about black dressing-gowns, camels in the desert,
what would happen if the bell rang during communion, runners
in Ceylon, the maid going through their drawers. The creative
energy which Katherine Mansfield put into literature is wasted
by them in pointless private fantasies. The most vivid of all are
those which concern the late Colonel, who, they fear, will come
back and accuse them of having him buried (and complain
about the bills; the fantasy is a very complete one), or who
perhaps is hiding in his chest of drawers. That conveys, better
than any direct statement, the fact that they were terrified of
him. The dutiful remarks ('We miss our dear father so much')
which they make even when they are alone together are
contradicted by the flurry of activity in their unconscious minds.
    They are middle-aged women – 'old tabbies' (2) to the young
maid – but the Colonel calls them 'girls', and their conversation
is very like children's:

'It can't be a mouse because there aren't any crumbs', said
Josephine.
'But it doesn't know there aren't', said Constantia.   (1)

Similarly when they are trying to force themselves to enter their father's room. 'You go first.' 'No, Jug, that's not fair. You're eldest.' 'But you're tallest' (6). The author is not 'poking fun at the poor old things',[90] as some readers thought; she felt nothing but sorrow for the two women who had never been allowed to grow up. Their lives have been spent 'arranging father's trays and trying not to annoy father' (12); they have been trained to talk about trivial things instead of their real preoccupations (the conversation about the meringues is a good example), and they are so unused to decision-making that they cannot even choose between fried and boiled fish. It is not funny but horrific. In the flashback (past flows into present, in this story, just as it does in people's minds) where their nephew visits them, his free life is contrasted with their subjection. The cake they feed him with stands for Josephine's 'winter gloves or the soling and heeling of Constantia's only respectable shoes', but having him there is 'one of their rare treats' (8). For Cyril and his father, the Colonel is not an ogre. It is only daughters who cannot leave home.

In the last section, they are able to believe that the Colonel has really gone, and begin to appreciate what he has done to them. 'If mother had lived, might they have married?' Now that he is no longer there, their minds can open briefly to more basic and soothing influences – music, sunlight, the moon and the sea. But it is too late. At the end, they have both forgotten what they were going to say because they cannot allow themselves to put their real problem into words.

Stories like this, and the slighter but still impressive 'Miss Brill', were based on the lives of women of Katherine Mansfield's class who had kept the rules and ended up despised and exploited. Along with the picture of Beryl in the 'Kezia' stories, they help us to understand why she herself had broken every rule rather than live like that. When she tried to enter a working-class woman's mind, in 'Life of Ma Parker', she was less successful, although it is still a moving piece of work. In her last few years of life, she wrote several stories – some of them among her best – about the gulf between rich and poor.

Ma Parker is a charwoman who works for a 'literary gentleman' – that is, one who does fairly trivial literary work like the narrator of 'Je ne parle pas français' or the people in 'Bliss'. Her feelings for him are more generous than his for her;

she pities him for having no one to look after him but he airily describes her as a 'hag' and suspects her of pinching his cocoa. Their very first conversation shows that he regards her as a creature of a different species:

> Then because these people set such store by funerals he said kindly, 'I hope the funeral went off all right'.
> 'Beg parding, sir?' said old Ma Parker huskily.

Words like 'parding', 'arsked', 'emigrimated', sound wrong because they fit too easily into the stereotype of a comic charwoman, while in fact the author takes Ma Parker very seriously. Even the name 'Ma' suggests that she has spent her whole life in the service of her family. But her only grandchild has died (to Katherine Mansfield, the relationship between grandmother and child was extremely basic) and she is left with absolutely nothing. Even the chance to express her grief is denied her because 'she had no right to cry in strangers' houses' and if she breaks down the police will want to know why.

The literary gentleman's 'warm sitting-room' is contrasted with the icy wind in the streets where Ma Parker is not permitted to cry. In the same way, in 'Revelations', the wind is contrasted with the artificial scents in the hairdresser's shop; Monica's suffering from her 'nerves' with the hairdresser's real pain. In 'The Garden Party' she wrote her most perfect story on this theme.

There had been a real garden party, when Katherine was a girl in Wellington with poor people living uncomfortably close to her parents' house. With her background, it was obviously much easier for her to write about the rich than about the poor, and the story does not attempt to deal directly with the family of the man who has been killed. The focus is firmly on the privileged Sheridans and the threat to their day of pleasure.

Interestingly enough, the Sheridan men are more compassionate than the women, whose only function is to give garden parties. Laura's sister says the correct things at first – 'I'm every bit as sorry about it as you. I feel just as sympathetic' – but when there is a real chance that the man's death could inconvenience her she becomes vicious: 'Her eyes hardened . . . . "You won't bring a drunken workman back to life by being sentimental", she said softly.'

Not surprisingly, Laura – who is defined, significantly, as 'the artistic one' – feels ill at ease with her family's values. Like the young Katherine Mansfield, she believes that 'one must go everywhere; one must see everything', so she deliberately explores the poor district near her home. She thinks she has risen above 'these absurd class distinctions', but of course she has not; it is a surprise to her that a workman should appreciate the smell of lavender. And although her conscience tells her that the party ought to be put off she enjoys it once it is happening; the vision of herself in a new hat blots out the picture of 'that poor woman and those little children and the body being carried into the house'.

Is the garden party simply an empty and heartless frolic, an example of conspicuous consumption, or is it, in some sense, a work of art? The image of the marquee blotting out the karaka trees ('proud, solitary, lifting their leaves and fruits to the sun in a kind of silent splendour') suggests the former. Yet the author can well understand the sensuous appeal of the Sheridans' way of life. The paragraph about the workmen's cottages says:

> The very smoke coming out of their chimneys was poverty-stricken. Little rags and shreds of smoke, so unlike the great silvery plumes that uncurled from the Sheridans' chimneys.

If even the Sheridans' smoke is an artefact, how much more so is everything to do with their garden party: passion-fruit ices, cream puffs, fifteen different kinds of sandwiches and above all the canna lilies which they can afford to buy in huge quantities. We are invited to marvel at the 'big pink flowers, wide open, radiant, almost frighteningly alive on bright crimson stems'. More important still are the women's hats – huge, frivolous, elaborate hats, traditionally worn by upper-class women to flaunt their spending power. It is her hat which distracts Laura from the accident and her hat which fills her with shame when she is confronted with the Scott family. Yet the hat (on whose velvet ribbons and gold daises the author dwells lovingly) is not evil in itself. In its small way, it too is a work of art.

The evil is in the attitude of Laura's mother, who finds it 'tactless' when people remind her of the accident and refers to the Scotts as 'people of that class'. Her assumption that they can be comforted by scraps from her party shows her utter disrespect for them. For Laura, they are 'nearly neighbours'. But, for all her real sympathy, Laura has to accept that the gulf between the classes cannot be bridged by a few friendly gestures. Whatever she does, the vast gap between those who enjoy the fullness of life, and those who have very little and die before their time, remains.

Katherine Mansfield continued to ponder this great difference in some of the last stories she wrote. The young couple in 'Honeymoon' are vaguely aware that other people are suffering but they can easily forget this; the man even gets a kick out of it. Rosemary Fell in 'A Cup of Tea' knows, like Laura, that she is privileged, but unlike Laura chooses to forget it:

> There are moments, horrible moments in life, when one emerges from shelter and looks out, and it's awful. One oughtn't to give way to them. One ought to go home and have an extra-special tea.

The author is severe with Rosemary, seeing her as a refined form of egoist (who incidentally patronises artists as 'quaint creatures'). She buys flowers (from a 'thin shop-girl') and expensive little enamel boxes not for the love of art but as a setting for herself. When she picks up the girl and gives her a meal she is conscious that she is doing something which 'she was always reading about or seeing on the stage'. This is true, of course, and most novelists who depict such scenes (e.g. Galsworthy in *Flowering Wilderness*) obviously feel that it enhances the heroine's status. But Rosemary is merely admiring her own behaviour. She assures the poor girl whose life is so different from her own that 'we're both women', but her theory that women are sisters is soon abandoned. When she realises that her husband finds the girl attractive, this shocks her, because ultimately her position depends on her keeping her sexual hold on him. She quickly dismisses the girl and retreats back into her shelter.

'The Doll's House' suggests that if there is anything which can bridge the gap between the classes, it can only be art. Kezia (the same character as in 'Prelude' and 'At the Bay'), is a member of the colonial upper class, but a fairly powerless one because she is a child, and a younger sister at that. The upper-class Burnells have to have some contact with the plebeian Kelveys because – and this is an unusual situation – they attend the same school. But the children have already learned the values of the adult world, and snub them mercilessly. Just as they do not question Isabel's precedence ('I'm to tell . . . because I'm the eldest'), so they – and their teacher – unthinkingly assume that they are better than the Kelveys, who are probably going to be servants. Here there is no pretence of being kind or charitable; the class conflict is quite naked. The children – the author says, unshocked – 'wanted to be horrid':

> 'Yah, yer father's in prison!' she hissed spitefully. This was such a marvellous thing to have said that the little girls rushed away in a body, deeply, deeply excited, wild with joy.

In the same way, Beryl – recognisably the same person as in 'At the Bay' – forgets her own problems and feels distinctly pleased with herself when she has 'frightened those little rats'.

Outside the narrow and nasty world of class snobbery, which reproduces itself under the most unlikely conditions, stands Kezia, who is Katherine Mansfield. She values the doll's house for quite different reasons from her friends, who see it only as a large and expensive toy. For her, the one part of the furniture which matters is the amber lamp, which is perfect, and represents art. 'Our Else' – the character was based on a washerwoman's child who loved painting – is the only one who shares her perception. When she says, 'I seen the little lamp', we realise that the class differences between the two girls are unimportant.

Katherine Mansfield wrote one more great story, 'The Fly'. Clearly, it was influenced by her brother's death and by the personality of her father, a 'boss' in New Zealand. We may also remember the character of Jonathan in 'At the Bay', whose office work makes him feel like a trapped insect. But perhaps the main inspiration came from *King Lear*:

> As flies to wanton boys, are we to the gods;
> They kill us for their sport.

Those lines must have taken on a new significance for a good many people during the Great War. 'The boy' and 'the boss' (they have no other names) are archetypal figures; symbols of the young men who died and the old men who dominate the commercial system. Yet 'the boss' has no control over life and death; his great aim has been to build up the business for his son, and now he is without one. The story is about his attempt to achieve a warped sort of power.

The first grief, the pure kind, does not last. Old Woodifield has got over his own son's death and is complaining about the price of jam. 'The boss' appears to have recovered too; he has surrounded himself with new furniture (to give himself a sense of his own importance) and when he tries to weep he cannot. This is the point at which he passes from mourning for his son to tormenting a fly. It is unpleasant and disturbing, and 'the boss' himself certainly does not understand the reasons for his action. The reader, aware that grief can take odd and twisted forms, may try to guess.

'The boss' stands in the same relation to the fly as the blind forces which started the war (what Shakespeare called 'the gods') did to his son. His experiment is not precisely sadistic; even while he drops ink on the creature he would prefer it to live. Probably he is aware that the war was a giant lottery; other men's sons had survived and if the fly does too this might, in some way, negate the death of the boy. But it dies, and he experiences a 'grinding feeling of wretchedness'. He has actually forgotten that the boy has been eliminated in the same pointless way – forgotten, because the pain is too great to be dealt with in his conscious mind.

Katherine Mansfield could, of course, only judge the war from its effects on civilians. In this small masterpiece – it is only six pages long – she made, perhaps, a more telling statement about the war's legacy than any number of histories and memoirs had done. By this time the cruelty of her early stories had gone and, although the subject-matter is about as depressing as it could be, the final effect is to extend our compassion. Just as Blake could see a world in a grain of sand, she was able to see the deaths of millions of men in the death of a fly.

A 'tiny talent'? Perhaps. It is certain that Katherine Mansfield deliberately chose to write only about what she understood and to weigh her words. 'I hate the sort of licence that English people give themselves – to spread over and flop and roll about', she wrote in 1913. 'I feel as fastidious as though I wrote with acid.'[91]

Her good stories might fill perhaps one slim volume, while many other writers turn out a million-word 'epic' every few years. Most of them are, or soon will be, forgotten. Katherine Mansfield is established as one of the great short-story writers of the world.

5

Dorothy L. Sayers

Dorothy Leigh Sayers was born on 13 June 1893 in Oxford, where her father, the Reverend Henry Sayers, was headmaster of Christ Church Choir School. She started life by being christened in the cathedral, and the traditional Oxford values of Anglicanism and scholarship did a great deal to form her personality. Her mother, born Helen Mary Leigh, had had a great-uncle who wrote for *Punch*. The humorist tradition had its effect on her too.

She would have had a more 'normal' upbringing, and been a different kind of person, if her parents had stayed in Oxford, a city she always loved. But when she was four the family moved to Bluntisham, Huntingdonshire, where her father became Rector. It was a small isolated village, in the fen country of great floods and marvellous churches where *The Nine Tailors* is set. Dorothy, an only child, grew up surrounded by doting adults and without any friends of her own age. Her most intense relationships were with books, not people. By the time she finally went to school (at Salisbury when she was fifteen) she was brilliant (she could already write poetry in French), eccentric, precocious, and doomed to unpopularity by her lack of social skills.

The school years were miserable. She blossomed when she won a scholarship in 1912 to Somerville College, Oxford, where she could mix with intelligent women like herself. In spite of leading an active social life, she got a First in modern languages, although as a woman she was not permitted to take her B.A. (she was one of the first batch of women to do so in 1920). She had considered doing research, but by this time the war had started and everyone was expected to do work of national importance. While other Somerville girls became nurses, sometimes overseas, she compromised by becoming a teacher at a girls' school in Hull. It was not a success, and she was soon back in Oxford working for Basil Blackwell. Over the next few years his firm published two volumes of her poems – one of them exclusively about religion.

Having gone through an adolescent crisis, she had emerged still a member of the Church of England, but in her own unconventional way. She had been much influenced by G. K. Chesterton, who saw Christianity as a dramatic, exciting world-view, not a tame and pious one. She was therefore quite happy to joke about certain kinds of religion and said in later life that she could only approach God through the intellect:

> I am quite incapable of 'religious emotion' . . . the lack of religious emotion in me makes me impatient of it in other people . . . . I have a moral sense. I am not sure that this derives from religious belief . . . . I do not enjoy it . . . . Of all the presuppositions of Christianity, the only one I really have and can swear to from personal inward conviction is sin.[92]

Her religion was an anchor in a post-war world in which so many traditional values had gone. She lost her job in 1919 and spent the next year working in France. Her parents were supportive, but she was determined not to go back to live in the Fens with them as a girl of an earlier generation might have done. While she was between jobs, it occurred to her that she could very probably make money by writing thrillers.

'The detective story of that period . . . enjoyed a pretty poor reputation', she wrote later. The academics among whom she had grown up assumed that 'a detective plot cannot bear any relation to a universal theme'. She hoped to make it 'become once more a novel of manners instead of a pure crossword puzzle'.[93] As a matter of fact she relished crossword puzzles and intellectual games of all kinds, but she also had serious preoccupations which inevitably found their way into her – very funny – novels. Knowing that the English love a lord, she created a titled sleuth, Lord Peter Wimsey, although she had absolutely no personal experience of aristocrats. Hard-up herself, she endowed him with a large unearned income.

Around this time began a series of unhappy relationships. Dorothy 'had practically never seen or spoken to any men of my own age till I was about twenty-five'.[94] There were not that many men available after the carnage of the war, and she was rather a plain woman. Her first real boy friend, whom she met after she had moved to Bloomsbury and begun to write *Whose Body?*, was a writer named John Cournos. Her professional life went well – the book was accepted and she got a congenial job as a copywriter in Benson's advertising agency – but the relationship was a disaster. Dorothy wanted marriage and children; he demanded an affair. She refused and stopped seeing him but, as she wrote some time later, 'both of us did what we swore we'd never do'.[95] On the rebound, she got involved with an unnamed man who shared none of her intellectual interests and in mid-1923 found herself pregnant.

A few years earlier she had persuaded a friend not to have an abortion and was not going to contemplate it in her own case. But she must have gone through agonies in the months that followed, wondering whether the man would marry her, whether she could avoid telling her family or losing her job. As it turned out, she covered her tracks like the skilled mystery writer she was. She never told her parents, friends or employers about the baby's existence, and the public did not find out until sixteen years after her death.

Her son, Anthony, was born on 3 January 1924. She left him with a cousin who looked after children for a small fee, and returned to Benson's. Her misery was intense around this time; for three years she spent most nights crying. But she continued to work and to write another novel, *Clouds of Witness*. The one permanent value, she now felt, was intellectual integrity.

Two years later her life improved when she met Captain Oswald Fleming – generally known as Mac – a journalist and former Special War Correspondent twelve years older than herself. They were married in April 1926, in a registry office (Mac had been divorced before she met him, which meant that she had to compromise her religious principles yet again). She hoped that Anthony would eventually be able to live with them as an 'adopted son', but after two years her husband's health began to decline, perhaps because of his experiences in the war. He became increasingly ill and irritable and rarely left the house they had bought at Witham, Essex. There was real affection between them but he must, like Teddy Wharton, have felt overshadowed by his wife as her fame grew. From then on

Dorothy kept her public and private lives strictly separate. Few people saw her with Mac; even fewer knew anything about her son.

She went on working for Benson's until 1930. She was a most valued member of their staff, writing some very successful slogans for Guinness and mustard, but she probably had secret doubts about the morality of what she was doing. In *Murder Must Advertise*, which is based on her work at the agency, the character most resembling herself says, 'My sort make nothing. We exploit other people's folly, take the cash and sneer at the folly. It's not admirable' (21). Eventually she became so popular in England and America that she felt free to concentrate on her own writing. As Q. D. Leavis noted disapprovingly, a few years later, she had 'stepped out of the ranks of detective writers into that of the best-seller novelists, and into some esteem as a literary figure among the educated reading public'.[96]

Although Lord Peter Wimsey was much loved by this public, his creator was getting tired of him. She wrote one novel, *The Documents in the Case* (1930), in which he does not appear, and which she called 'a serious "criticism of life" so far as it goes'.[97] In the same year she published *Strong Poison*, which had been begun with the intention of 'marrying him off and getting rid of him',[98] and which introduced a new character, Harriet Vane, who was very like herself. In fact the Wimsey novels went on appearing until *Busman's Honeymoon* in 1937.

After that she virtually began a new career. Her play *The Zeal of Thy House*, performed in 1937 in Canterbury Cathedral, quickened her interest in drama and religious matters. In the early years of the war she wrote *The Man Born to be King*, a series of radio plays on the life of Jesus which were very popular, aiming as they did to make the Gospel seem meaningful to the ordinary person. She broadcast and wrote about theology, the war and the position of women; her views ranging from the thoughtful to the simply silly. She was associated with other religious intellectuals such as C. S. Lewis, Charles Williams and (to a lesser extent) T. S. Eliot. The Church of England offered her a Doctorate of Divinity, which she refused. But she often appeared in public (not always with much pleasure) as a Christian controversialist.

Her last great enthusiasm was Dante, whom she discovered – at that time she knew no Italian – in 1944. She agreed to translate the *Divine Comedy* into English verse for Penguin Classics, an enormous job which took her the rest of her life. Her husband died in 1950. She had spent a good deal of time looking after him, and wrote rather sadly that 'it seems impossible there should be so many uninterrupted hours in the day'.[99] Two volumes of the *Divine Comedy* appeared in her lifetime, but the third was still unfinished when she died, very suddenly, on 17 December 1957.

Dorothy Sayers did not personally get closer to the First World War than being bombed by Zeppelins in Hull. But, like most people who had lived through it, she felt that it had profoundly altered the texture and quality of life. In *The Documents in the Case*, a clergyman (and clergymen are always treated with respect in her novels) who is asked what has made his job most difficult, says: 'The War . . . . It has taken the heart out of people . . . made it easy to believe and difficult not to believe – in anything. Just anything' (52).

The novels she wrote in the 1920s and 1930s are peopled by wounded or shell-shocked men and working women who no longer believe in pre-war values – neither religion nor traditional morality. What this means can best be expressed by saying that, before the war, it would have been almost impossible for a girl of Dorothy's background to have had an illegitimate child. Colonel Marchbanks in *The Unpleasantness at the Bellona Club*, a sympathetic character, suggests that

the War has had a bad effect on some of our young men . . . . I certainly notice a less fine sense of honour in these days than we had when I was a boy. There were not so many excuses made then for people; there were things that were done and things that were not done. Nowadays men – and, I am sorry to say, women too – let themselves go in a way that is to me quite incomprehensible. (22)

Dorothy probably agreed with most of this, but she did not find the new order incomprehensible. She was conscious of a great gap between her own generation and that which had grown up before the war. Her public pose, in her early novels, was that of a cynical woman of the world. In the same book, she made jokes about poppies and the two minutes' silence which must have offended many readers. The hero of her story 'Blood Sacrifice' writes an angry and iconoclastic play about the war's effect on people's natures, and then has to alter it so that an audience which wants to hear about heroism and pure women will find it acceptable. How she would have developed if she had tried to write 'straight' fiction we do not know. But if we read Katherine Mansfield's reviews of the truly dreadful novels which were coming out week by week in 1919 and 1920, we can see just how much was wrong with the post-war literary scene, and how good a writer, by comparison, Dorothy Sayers was. She did not usually claim that her work was 'a serious criticism of life', but she did use it, repeatedly, to make serious points.

The same is true of her great contemporary, Agatha Christie. They wrote different kinds of crime novel; Agatha Christie does not reveal the murderer's identity till the last moment, while in Sayers novels it is often obvious; Dorothy was an intellectual while Agatha Christie was not. But their attitude to crime was very similar. They did not glorify it; neither woman could have created a hero like James Bond who is as amoral as the people he is fighting. One Christie character says:

> I believe at least in one of the chief tenets of the Christian faith – *contentment with a lowly place*. I am a doctor and I know that ambition – the desire to succeed – to have power – leads to most ills of the human soul. If the desire is realised it leads to arrogance, violence and final satiety – and if it is denied – ah! if it is denied – let all the asylums for the insane rise up and give their testimony![100]

Dorothy Sayers never put it quite so bluntly, but that was essentially her own attitude. Some of her murderers are the victims of circumstance but others act out of pure arrogance. Mary Whittaker, in *Unnatural Death*, apparently thinks 'that anyone who inconvenienced her had no right to exist' (23). In the same novel, a perceptive clergyman says that 'the damage to Society, the wrongness of the thing lies much more in the harm it does the killer than in anything it can do to the person who is killed', and stresses that we have no right to 'take life and death into our hands' (19). Her first novel, *Whose Body?*, examines this thesis at some length.

Her purpose is not to tease us about the murderer's identity; that is obvious from an early stage. It is to display, in bizarre detail, the perverted psychology of Sir Julian Freke. A freak in every sense, he is not willing to be one of the normal, kindly, slightly ridiculous men who inhabit the rest of the novel. He insists on being looked up to as a great scientist (his attacks on his opponents are savage) and, after his death, a great criminal. The author makes it clear that he is indeed a great man, whose patients revere him and who has a vast potential for good. His face is 'beautiful, impassioned and inhuman' (11); we are reminded of the fallen angel Lucifer. Religion is a delusion, in his view, and 'conscience is a sort of vermiform appendix. Chop it out and you'll feel all the better' (10). He 'cuts people up . . . could take you or me to pieces like a clock' (9); the human body is merely a sophisticated machine to him. Like Raskolnikov, he sees himself as a superman and the vast mass of fellow-humans as worthless creatures over whom he has the power of life and death. 'There appeared to me to be no object in indefinitely prolonging so unprofitable an existence' (13), he writes of the tramp whom he kills. Yet, in the end, he is brought down by his own high opinion of himself. He loses the chance to commit suicide which Wimsey sportingly offers him, and is hanged, because he cannot resist writing a confession which dwells lovingly on the gruesome details.

His opponent, Lord Peter Wimsey, has to be something of a superman himself to bring Freke down. Q. D. Leavis described him as 'a distinguished scholar in history, a celebrated cricketer, an authority on antiques, a musician, a brilliant wit, a diplomat on whom the F.O. leans during international crises, a wide and deep reader and no doubt some other things I've overlooked.'[101] (She could have added, a specialist in unarmed combat, a high diver, a campanologist and a creator of first-rate advertising slogans.) We may well get annoyed with Wimsey, partly because the author is too prone to think that women find him irresistible, partly because we feel that he is indecently privileged compared to the other struggling people we meet in her bleak post-war world. But he does have two qualities which bring him nearer to common humanity; he has been shell-shocked, and he feels guilty about his relation to those less privileged than himself. He often wonders whether he is entitled to be a private detective, knowing that this will lead to men being hanged (Munting in *The Documents in the Case* has the same dilemma). In our last glimpse of Wimsey, in *Busman's Honeymoon*, he is close to a nervous breakdown for this reason. Parker reminds him that he has a 'duty to society', and that he is not an overgrown public schoolboy but 'a responsible person' (*Whose Body?*, 7) (the sense of responsibility is merely a physiological reaction to Sir Julian Freke). The suggestion is that only those who are squeamish about using power are fit to have it.

Wimsey has the same problem in *Unnatural Death*. Once again the murderer is an arrogant person who feels, like Milton's Satan, that it is 'better to reign in hell than serve in heaven' (16). Should he leave this person alone or speak out, for the sake of abstract justice? The question is not easy to answer, because his investigations lead to more deaths. In this book the criminal is a woman, and an 'unnatural' woman at that. Mary Whittaker has a 'masculine understanding' (18) – not a bad thing in itself – and is called 'sexless' and 'spinsterish' (15) because she is indifferent to men. She prefers to control the lives of chickens and the young girl Vera Findlater. We may feel it is sexist of Lord Peter to assume that Mary is a freak merely because she does not find him attractive. It would be quite wrong, though, to think that this novel is an attack on spinsters.

As is noted at an early stage, there are two million 'surplus females' in England of the 1920s. *Unnatural Death* marks the first appearance of the 'experienced spinster' Miss Climpson, who is a natural sleuth. We learn later from *Strong Poison* that Wimsey finances a bureau, staffed by her and other spinsters, whose job is to track down the men who live off unprotected women, so perhaps he is a more useful member of society than he appears. This is how he describes their detective talents:

Thousands of old maids, simply bursting with useful energy, forced by our stupid social system into hydros and hotels and communities and hostels and posts as companions, where their magnificent gossip-powers and units of inquisitiveness are allowed to dissipate themselves or even become harmful to the community, while the ratepayers' money is spent on getting work for which these women are providentially fitted, inefficiently carried out by ill-equipped policemen.' (3)

Miss Climpson is much the same kind of person as the more famous Miss Marple (who, however, was invented later). The tone is light but it is perfectly true that countless women of her type are wasted. She says she might have 'made a very good lawyer' (3), but was denied an education by an old-fashioned father. She has led a 'woman-ridden life' (22) in cheap boarding-houses and knows about the kind of emotional desolation which other lonely women suffer. They are either frantic to find a man, or unhealthily absorbed in another woman, a kind of relationship which is born out of frustration and is destructive: '*Men* . . . find it easier to give and take in that way – probably because they have so many outside interests' (16). Miss Climpson is saved from a fate like this by her religion (which is meant to be taken seriously, in spite of some extravagances) and because she gets the chance to use her brain. She is, incidentally, 'a perfectly womanly woman' (16), who might have preferred to marry but is quite capable of leading a useful life as a celibate. Several years later, Dorothy Sayers was to write a whole novel as a tribute to such women.

The Documents in the Case is another novel about a woman criminal, this time a completely different type from Mary Whittaker and one who is not made to pay for her crime. We have Dorothy Sayers's word that it was meant to be 'a serious "criticism of life"', and it benefits from not including Wimsey among the characters. It is told, like an eighteenth-century novel, in letters, but the subject-matter – life in a London suburb in the 1920s – is entirely contemporary. The device works very well, showing as it does how people with quite different assumptions co-exist.

The world is changing, and the suburbs have not yet realised it. Two young men, a serious novelist and a serious painter, move into Bayswater where their work is considered 'unpleasant' or 'shocking'. Their neighbour, Harrison, does bad paintings in his spare time and believes that a woman's place is in the home. His wife, a suburban vamp, does nothing but read cheap novels. 'The period from which we are emerging was like no other', Dorothy Sayers wrote some ten years later, 'a period when empty head and idle hands were qualities for which a man prized his woman.'[102] Having no 'moral standards of her own' (37), she gets her image of herself from novels and newspapers which reflect the fact that she is living in a time of transition, posing as a professional woman, courtesan or nun as the fancy takes her. Lathom, the complete Bohemian, remarks that people in the suburbs 'believe in Respectability' and will 'lie, die, commit murder to keep up appearances' (37). This is precisely what Margaret Harrison does; since divorce is unacceptable in her circle she (in effect) condemns her husband to death rather than have people think badly of her.

Dorothy Sayers identifies herself with the new trends in art and literature (some of her own work could certainly be called 'unpleasant'), but she does not dismiss the old morality. Munting, who considers himself a modern, instinctively falls back on the 'foolish shibboleths about honour and self-sacrifice' (37) when he senses that his friend Lathom is behaving badly. Harrison is absurd in many ways but a decent man and, more important, he has a right to live. On the other hand Lathom is a fine painter but, like Sir Julian Freke, ruthlessly dismissive of the claims of others. 'It is fatally easy for a man like that to imagine that the ordinary rules of morality do not apply to him' (20), as Harrison says in another context. Mrs Harrison, too, is quickly learning to be a 'modern' type, but not one that the author or anyone else can admire.

Serious women novelists do not usually have much sympathy with vamps, and Dorothy Sayers has none for Margaret Harrison. From the moment she begins to hold forth about 'poetry and imagination and the beautiful things of the mind' (9), she is established as a stupid woman (contrasted, I think, with Munting's wife, who is self-supporting and a serious novelist). Possibly the author allowed her to escape any punishment because she thought, cynically, that such women always did. Her letters are a mixture of sickly sentiment and utter selfishness. Although she is not in fact prepared to acknowledge what she is doing, she likes to play with the idea of herself as 'free and splendid and ready to proclaim her splendid passion to the world' (37). The author seems to be criticising D. H. Lawrence (Lathom encourages his mistress to read *Women in Love*) for teaching that 'passion' is the ultimate good. A crude version of this idea has trickled down to Margaret, who writes:

how true and right it was that the useless husband should be got out of the way of the living, the splendid wife and her

> lover and child . . . that's Nature's law . . . get rid of the ugly
> and sick and weak and worn-out things, and let youth and
> love and happiness have their chance.   (43)

But if it is 'nature's law' that the weak and 'useless' should be
'got rid of', there is also a moral law which cannot be flouted
with impunity. The clergyman is quoted on the same page:

> he said, if we wouldn't do as the Gospel said, and keep good
> for the love of God, then we should be punished by the Law.
> And he said that didn't mean that God was vindictive, only
> that the Laws of Nature had their way, and worked out the
> punishment quite impartially, just as fire burns you if you
> touch it.   (43)

The idea that certain elemental forces will punish the evil-doer
is developed further in *The Nine Tailors*. Meanwhile, Lathom is
punished by the law (in the literal sense) because he overlooked
a fundamental law of nature. The climax of the novel is a tough
metaphysical discussion, not at all what readers of thrillers
normally expect, about the origins and meaning of life. Out of
this emerges the clue which hangs Lathom, and the need for
Munting to make a particularly painful choice. Science and
ethics, apparently, cannot be separated. But Dorothy Sayers
was too intelligent to claim that human beings in a fallen world
could expect more than rough justice. 'Unfortunately, the
sinner isn't always the victim . . . . We suffer for one another,
as, indeed, we must, being all members one of another' (52).

Her next novel, *Strong Poison*, continued the theme that
women in the post-war world were exposed to conflicting sets of
values. It had been begun with the intention of finding a wife
for Peter Wimsey, but that was not how it worked out. Harriet
Vane, the author said, was 'a human being from the start'.[103]
As a young woman who supported herself by writing detective
stories, she bore an obvious likeness to Dorothy Sayers. But the
novel's first readers could not know that Dorothy's life resembled
Harriet's in certain other very relevant ways. Harriet is on trial
not just for murder but for having had a lover; her public
ordeal mirrors Dorothy's private ordeal in 1923–4. The hurt
which she suffers for years afterwards is precisely what Dorothy
herself must have felt.

Harriet has been 'brought up on strictly religious principles' (like Dorothy) but got involved with a man of 'advanced' ideas who nagged her into living with him. To the judge, she is guilty of 'an ordinary, vulgar act of misbehaviour' (1). Neither he, nor the kindly, puzzled clergyman, nor Philip Boyes himself, can understand why, 'after all that had passed between them' (6), she refused to marry him. Modern and conventional ideas appear to clash but are actually quite similar. Harriet is a liberated woman not because she agreed to live with her lover (there is no suggestion that this did her any good) but because she broke with him when she realised that he was exploiting her. 'Philip wasn't the sort of man to make a friend of a woman. He wanted devotion', she says (4). What this means is spelled out by their friends, 'You'd think it would have been enough for her to help and look after a genius like Phil' and 'She ought to have been ministering to his work, not making money for them both with her own independent trash' (8). His work is taken more seriously by all concerned than hers is. Women geniuses, as a feminist friend says grimly, do not expect to be looked after.

Although she takes an active part in later novels, Harriet, stuck in her prison cell, cannot help to solve the mystery in this one. The bulk of the detective work is done by Miss Climpson (who also shows herself an independent woman by refusing to be bullied into giving the wrong verdict). Wimsey gets the credit for saving her, but he is not allowed to marry her yet. For, as she worked on the novel, Dorothy Sayers realised that Harriet would have been a disappointingly conventional heroine if she had simply dropped into his arms on the last page. 'I could find no form of words in which she could accept him without loss of self-respect.'[104]

In the next novel about Harriet, *Have his Carcase*, she continued to stress that women must be prepared to live independently of men if necessary. The pathetic middle-aged Mrs Weldon – who has 'lived for my emotions' (5) and not been taught to do anything constructive – is a frightening example of what can happen to women who are desperate to capture a man, any man.

But her next few novels abandoned the Harriet story. In her later writings, the stress on the human need to do useful and satisfying work became more and more emphatic. The artists in

Five Red Herrings, who 'take their work seriously and have no time for amateurs' (1), and go fishing in their spare time, are one example of a group of people who live in a healthy way. Others are the Fen village-dwellers in *The Nine Tailors* and the Oxford scholars in *Gaudy Night*. Contrasted with them are the unreal worlds of pseudo-literary London, advertising and the Bright Young Things. She suggested, in *Murder Must Advertise*, that the last two are equally vicious, and linked both with the drug trade. There is hardly any hint in this book that any other way of life is possible, which is perhaps the reason why it makes depressing reading. *The Nine Tailors*, by contrast, is a masterpiece.

For this novel, she drew deeply on her memories of her Fen childhood, the ancient churches, bell-ringing (contrasted favourably with the sounds of jazz and cars), floods. History is written all over this flat landscape, in ditches, box-tombs with rhyming epitaphs, the three-hundred-year-old pit dug for Tailor Paul. There are references to the war, and a hint that things have been 'topsy-turvy' ever since (2,2), but human memory goes much further back, to the draining of the Fens, Cromwell, Abbot Thomas, the pre-Christian carvings in the church and beyond. Then there are the complicated and beautiful rituals of bell-ringing and the liturgy, which could be considered unchanging and eternal. But, to her urban readers, the custom of tolling the bell every time a parishioner died ('nine tailors make a man') must already have seemed archaic. It implies a small, organic community, in which every person is intimately known and valued, and the London crooks who invade this community (Deacon, significantly, is not a local man) do not understand its ways.

The social structure of Fenchurch St Paul seems almost feudal. Railways and cars do exist but virtually everyone attends church and people say 'sir', 'my lord', 'my man'. One of the bell-ringers even speaks of doing 'our dooties in the station whereto we are called' (2,2). The Thorpe family at the local great house are sympathetic characters and when Lady Thorpe dies it is a 'calamity' for the parish. Dorothy Sayers had some admiration for the English landed gentry, saying in her spoof biography of Wimsey that their 'underlying sense of social responsibility' kept them from being 'a total loss, spiritually speaking'. The fact that the Thorpes are impoverished and have to go away can be blamed partly on the war and

partly on individual greed. However, even when the great house
has been broken up, the Church remains a positive force. The
Rector takes a sick woman to hospital, organises flood relief,
and is generally a devoted pastor. The fact that the nameless
corpse gets a Christian funeral and the bell tolled for him
underlines the point that this is a community where everything
is done decently and in order.

It is tempting, then, to see the church as a symbol of kindness
and civilisation, particularly near the end when it becomes a
kind of Noah's ark fighting the storm. But religion has other
aspects, and they can be terrifying. Cranton, when he is in the
church at night for no good purpose, feels as if 'hundreds of
eyes' were watching him (these would be the angels in the
roof), thinks that the bells are alive, and finally falls into a ditch
of cold water and is invalided for life. (3,2). Bells and the 'slow,
unforgiving waters' (1,1) are the most powerful presences in the
novel. The flood executes rough justice at the end when Will
Thoday (and another man) are drowned, because he bears
some responsibility for the death of Deacon. But, as we do not
learn until the last page, it was the bells that really killed him.

There is no human murderer in this book, apart from Deacon,
fleeing from justice and avid for money. Behind all the
skulduggery about emerald necklaces, there is the serious point
that Deacon was a bad man and that we interfere with certain
powerful forces at our peril. The bells have already killed two
men and, the Rector speculates, 'perhaps God speaks through
those mouths of inarticulate metal. He is a righteous judge,
strong and patient, and is provoked every day' (4,3). Or, as the
slightly unreal rustic Hezekiah says:

> 'They can't abide a wicked man. They lays in wait to
> overthrow 'un . . . . Make righteousness your course bell, my
> lord, an' keep a-follerin' on her an' she'll see you through
> your changes till Death calls you to stand. Yew ain't no call
> to be afeared o' the bells if so be as yew follows righteousness.'
> 'Oh, quite', said Wimsey, a little embarrassed.   (3,1)

The author's sense of humour did not often desert her.
Nevertheless, in this her best novel, she is straining the
conventional detective story to its limits.

Like many intelligent women, Dorothy Sayers was in two minds about feminism. She had personally encountered prejudice of the crudest kind, when she was prevented from taking her degree on the grounds of her sex, and she was committed to legal equality and to a woman's right to do any job for which she was qualified. But she said in 1938 that 'an aggressive feminism might do more harm than good'.[105] She was what was known between the wars as an 'old feminist', as opposed to the 'new feminists' who were chiefly concerned with women's 'special' or 'biological' needs. Attempts to prove that women were a homogeneous block – 'that *all* one's tastes and prejudices have to be conditioned by the class to which one belongs'[106] – annoyed her. On the contrary, she argued, each woman had her own personality and interests and was entitled to be treated as a human, not a sexual being:

> I am occasionally desired ... to say something about the writing of detective fiction 'from the woman's point of view'. To such demands, one can only say, 'Go away and don't be silly. You might as well ask what is the female angle on an equilateral triangle'.[107]

This is part of the background of ideas which we should be aware of when reading *Gaudy Night*, the last of her good novels and the one which examines the 'woman question' at greatest length. We also need to know that spinsters came in for a great deal of open hostility during the 1920s. Constraints on sexual behaviour were loosening; Freudianism and 'sex reform' were becoming fashionable. Celibate women, who had never been treated with much respect at any time, were now told by various experts that they were denying their essential womanly nature and doing themselves fearful harm:

> the concept of the 'prude' ... was refined during the 1920s with the aid of psychoanalytical 'insights' about repression .... It was asserted that 'repression' of the supposedly innate and powerful sexual urge would cause that urge to find its outlet in a lurid interest in things sexual disguised as disgust and condemnation.[108]

These 'insights' had filtered their way down, via the press, into popular consciousness. So when there is an outbreak of poison-pen letters in a women's college, even Harriet, who ought to know better, assumes that a female scholar must be responsible. 'The warped and repressed mind is apt enough to turn and wound itself. "Soured virginity" – "unnatural life" – "semi-demented spinsters" – "starved appetites and suppressed impulses" – "unwholesome atmosphere" – she could think of whole sets of epithets, ready-minted for circulation' (*Gaudy Night*, 4). Unless we are reading very carefully, we are liable to miss the irony.

Repressed spinsters did exist, of course. Miss Hillyard in this novel is one example, and there is another in *The Documents in the Case*. But, like Miss Climpson, the majority of Oxford women come through their time of stress very well. The real criminal (there is no murder) is not a spinster but a traditional woman who has no respect for the intellect and upholds the claims of 'my man, right or wrong' (17). By contrast, the fellows of Shrewbsury College are all women who are capable of making moral judgements. 'The University is a Paradise' because it stands for the permanent value of intellectual integrity (as opposed to cocktail party culture and its Book of the Fortnight or Book of the Moment). Women are newcomers to the university, are poor compared to the men and are not always confident about themselves, but they are still part of a great tradition. They can even improve on it, since they have the usual womanly virtue of concern for other people, such as the college employees. 'Nobody's interests ever seemed to be overlooked or forgotten, and an endless goodwill made up for a perennial scarcity of funds' (3).

Women at that time usually felt that they had to choose between a career and marriage. The Shrewsbury dons have all chosen to be single (in Miss de Vine's case, after a struggle, because she realised that she was too absorbed in her work to be a conventionally good wife). Today quite a few would be married, but in other ways the intellectual climate of *Gaudy Night* seems very familiar. There are the arguments, which we still hear, about taking jobs from men, about who the exceptional woman can marry, about whether working and having children can be combined. We meet a clever woman who has been swallowed up by marriage, an unsupported mother who has to keep leaving work when her child is ill, and another woman

who is happily combining marriage and career. This is the
ideal, especially for those who happen to be 'cursed with both a
heart and a brain' (9).

The whole point of the novel is that spinster dons are not
neurotic but creative women, whose interests are 'directed
immediately to God and His universe, not intermediately
through any child of man'.[109] And the author insists that it is
quite possible to do without personal relationships: 'Don't
stampede yourself into them by imagining that you've got to
have them or qualify for a Freudian case-book' (15). But the
fellows of Shrewsbury are not hostile to married women; indeed
they are sometimes accused of having an inferiority complex
about them. And it is surely significant that Harriet, who is
Dorothy, does finally agree to marry Wimsey at the end of the
book, once she is sure that he respects her as an equal. She
dreams of him in language very like that of women's magazines –
'drowsing and floating up out of the strong circle of his arms,
through a green sea of sun-dappled beech-leaves' (6). It was a
pity that Dorothy could not resist making Wimsey a sex-object
(unlike Agatha Christie, who had no difficulty in showing
Poirot as simultaneously a brilliant detective and a comic little
man). The sequel, *Busman's Honeymoon*, the weakest and most
self-indulgent of her books, contains 'romantic' writing that is
worse still.

Yet perhaps Dorothy Sayers did suspect that Wimsey was an
unreal figure. Annie, who makes out an impressive case for the
traditional 'stand by your man' philosophy, tells him:

> It's men like you that make women like this . . . . What do
> you know about life with your title and your money and your
> clothes and motor-cars? You've never done a hand's turn of
> honest work. You can buy all the women you want. Wives
> and mothers may rot and die for all you care, while you
> chatter about duty and honour. (22)

She has a point. It is a real criticism of Wimsey and the
Senior Common Room that they are stunned by a display of
naked emotion and have no idea how working-class women
have to live. Yet, ultimately, Dorothy Sayers felt that blind love
and hate were destructive, and that men and women could only
find real satisfaction through being 'true to one's calling,

whatever follies one might commit in one's emotional life' (2). Annie is stunting her daughters (telling the child who wants to keep a garage that she *has* to be a wife and mother) by her narrow conception of what women may do. By contrast, Miss de Vine is an unlikeable character, and admits that she is profoundly uninterested in her fellow human beings. Yet, like the characters in earlier detective novels who decide that justice must come before personal loyalties, she is observing some kind of moral law.

It will be seen that *Gaudy Night*, with its loose structure and its profound questioning of assumptions, is a world away from the simple puzzle stories which the younger Dorothy Sayers had written. Here she is not asking *who*, or even *how*, but, much more fundamentally, *why?* It was her last novel that mattered, for after the mid-1930s her interests turned to drama and the translation of Dante. We may regret that she did not write more detective stories, or switch to 'serious' novels. But we would be unwise to think that the novels we have are merely 'entertainment'.

6

Antonia White

Antonia White, whose real name was Eirene Adeline Botting, was born in Kensington on 31 March 1899. Her father, Cecil Botting, had raised himself through scholarships from a very ordinary background to become a classics master at St Paul's School. He was very much the dominant figure in the early life of his only child; years later she wrote: 'He centred everything on me, trying to force me into an exact replica of himself. I adored him, feared him and was never at ease with him.'[110] Her mother, born Christine White, was pretty, pleasure-loving and had little interest in children. Antonia's relationship with her was not nearly so deep and intense.

A great bookworm, she spent a lot of time reading in the nursery while her parents were occupied elsewhere. Unlike most middle-class children at that time, she got virtually no religious instruction, but that changed abruptly in 1906 when Cecil Botting was converted to Catholicism. This made it impossible for him to get any further in his profession; his example taught his daughter that religion was the most important thing in life, and that it demanded sacrifices. Christine also joined the Church, mainly under his influence. Antonia, a bright child of seven, quickly learned the fundamentals of her new creed. Soon afterwards her father, wishing her to be educated in a wholly Catholic atmosphere, sent her as a boarder to the Convent of the Sacred Heart, Roehampton.

It is necessary to read her novel *Frost in May* to get the full flavour of this experience. She worked hard and accepted the Catholic faith unquestioningly, but she was always conscious that as a convert she was different from her schoolmates. Moreover, as Mary McCarthy, who was educated at a sister convent, writes, 'Sacred Heart girls were not *ordinary* Catholics

98

but daughters of the best families';[111] compared with them,
Antonia felt poor and provincial. It was taken for granted that
most of them would marry young, have large families, and
never need to work. She on the other hand was expected to go
to Cambridge, as her father had done, and then earn her own
living, probably as a teacher.

Her time at the convent ended dramatically in her early
teens when the nuns discovered a juvenile novel of hers and
showed it to her father. He was furious, told her that she was
impure and corrupt, and took her away. In later years he was
never willing to discuss what had happened. This may seem
fairly trivial; in fact it was one of the most traumatic events of
her life.

'In a mild way', she 'behaved outrageously'[112] at St Paul's
Girls' School, which she attended next. She did little work,
went out with young officers on leave (although she was quite
indifferent to the war) and tried writing cosmetic advertisements.
The makers were happy to pay for them; she discovered while
still in her teens that she could make good money with very
little effort. She refused to go to university and tried various
jobs, teaching and working as a clerk at the Ministry of
Pensions; then took a drama course and did a tour in the
provinces. Soon afterwards, in 1921, she married a young man
from a rich family, Reggie Green-Wilkinson, of whom her father
highly approved.

The story of that marriage and its aftermath is told in *The
Sugar House* and *Beyond the Glass*. Reggie was 'sweet but
hopelessly reckless and feckless and an incurable drinker'.[113]
The marriage was never consummated and was eventually
annulled by the Catholic Church. While waiting for this to
happen she fell seriously in love with a young officer. Then,
with practically no warning, she became insane and spent nine
months in Bedlam. Her experiences included being forcibly fed
and kept in a padded cell. When, against all expectation, she
recovered the man had married someone else.

This is where *Beyond the Glass* leaves Clara, Antonia's *alter ego*.
But the real Antonia still had to live through many experiences,
some of them bizarre. In 1924 she got a job at Crawford's
advertising agency, rising to be their head woman copywriter.
In the same year she made another strange marriage, to a civil
servant, Eric Earnshaw Smith (Clive Heron in her books).

Their relationship was close and affectionate, but platonic. She ceased to practise her religion and became more involved with the literary world, writing and publishing a few serious short stories and helping to edit a small magazine. Then in 1928 she met an engineer, Silas Glossop, became pregnant by him, and took steps to get her second marriage annulled.

Her daughter, the future novelist Susan Chitty, was born in August 1929. Later in the year Antonia's father died, bitterly disappointed by the way she had rejected his values. The baby was left in a children's home and Antonia returned to Crawford's. Here she met Tom Hopkinson, a young copywriter who wanted to be a novelist and journalist. In future years he would be editor of *Picture Post*. After much agonising, and without getting the approval of the Church, she married him instead of Susan's father, in November 1930. Their daughter, Lyndall, named after the heroine of the *African Farm*, was born the following year.

The children saw very little of their mother. They lived in a separate part of the Kensington flat, looked after by a nurse, while Antonia freelanced. She was working full-time when she wrote her most famous novel, *Frost in May*. Later she said that she had found it very difficult to do any serious creative writing while her father was alive, and that she had relied heavily on her husband's encouragement. It was published in 1933 and got enthusiastic reviews. She left Crawford's and took various other jobs, among them fashion editor of the *Daily Mirror*, but was always hard up. The obvious next step was to write a second novel, and she tried to do so, but emotional difficulties blocked her way.

Antonia was not an easy woman to live with. She was extravagant, lost her temper easily, and her mental balance was uncertain. Now the success of *Frost in May* had a damaging effect on her marriage and sanity. 'I was not happy', Tom Hopkinson writes, 'to be introduced at parties as "the husband of Tony White who's just written that marvellous book". I longed to achieve some success of my own.'[114] As he withdrew emotionally, and became involved with another woman, she began to fear that she was going mad again. She went to live alone and had several years of Freudian analysis, which, she felt, was:

remarkably successful in removing the agonising obsessions and fears and making me capable of managing my life at least tolerably reasonably . . . . I can never be grateful enough either to the analyst himself or to Freud who laid the foundations of analysis. It is open to Catholics to say that if I had practised my religion I should never have got into the state of mind which needed analysis. To which I can only reply that before my first breakdown I had never even remotely considered ceasing to be a Catholic.[115]

She was able to go on working as a journalist and copywriter during this time, and then to move back to live with her children. (They also spent long periods of time with their father and later at boarding school.) She was divorced from Tom Hopkinson in 1938. A series of brief relationships after the break-up of her marriage led nowhere. At the end of 1940, living alone in wartime London and doing an uncongenial job with the BBC, she suddenly decided to go back to the Catholic Church. Her account of this experience, published much later in *The Hound and the Falcon*, shows that she did so with mixed feelings.

'If you have a double nature, you cannot expect a peaceful life',[116] she wrote around this time. Her life had not been peaceful, and she had an intense love–hate relationship with her religion. For the last fifteen years she had been mixing with liberal intellectuals who took for granted many things the Church condemned, yet she had not been able to free herself from its emotional pull. 'So far', she wrote in 1942, 'I have not found anyone who understands both languages.'[117] She hesitated for some time about practising a religion which seemed to her to be 'poetically' true, but perhaps not literally: 'I think religion oversteps its function in claiming to be literally true. It seems to me a religion should be a *method* of exploring the realm of spirit.'[118] She also confessed that 'the hardest article of faith for me to swallow is that God loves human beings'.[119]

Nevertheless, she did remain within the Catholic Church for the rest of her life and did not go mad again. She continued to live alone or with her two daughters. After the war she just managed to make an income by translating novels from French, eventually bringing out more than thirty, and also wrote articles and book reviews. Her own writing hung fire until, after more psychiatric help, she began work on *The Lost Traveller,* an unacknowledged sequel to *Frost in May.*

It depressed her that people knew her only as the author of that one novel. When *The Lost Traveller* appeared, in 1950, it had a mixed reception; one critic saying 'that she could not understand how this piece of woman's magazine rubbish came from the pen of the author of *Frost in May*'.[120] Two more novels based on her early life, *The Sugar House* and *Beyond the Glass,* came out in 1952 and 1954. She tried for many years to complete the story of Clara, but only managed to do four chapters:

> She teased a sentence like a cat with a mouse, until the page was black with crossings out and rewritings. She claimed that translating had made her cease to know what was her own style, and she remembered with nostalgia the ease with which she had written *Frost in May.* Often one barely legible page was all she had to show for a morning's work.[121]

As she grew older she lived more and more in the past. The three novels written in the 1950s had described the events of thirty years earlier; in her seventies, she tried to write about her childhood, but in spite of years of work could not get beyond the age of four. By this time her novels had gone out of print and, apart from *Frost in May,* been forgotten. In the late 1970s, though, Virago reprinted all four in their Modern Classics series. Readers and critics were greatly impressed, and they are now recognised as minor masterpieces. They were dramatised as a four-part series on BBC television in 1981, but Antonia did not live to see it. She died, aged eighty-one, at a nursing-home in Sussex run by nuns, on 10 April 1980.

Inevitably, *Frost in May* has been compared to James Joyce's *Portrait of the Artist as a Young Man.* Antonia had read it and been 'profoundly disturbed and influenced'[122] by it (especially the hellfire sermon). But it is doubtful whether she actually learned anything from Joyce; in spite of differences of sex and country, each had endured the full rigours of a Catholic education and had no need to borrow their subject-matter from anyone else. Antonia White is much the more accessible writer, particularly for women (perhaps the long years spent in advertising had helped her to be a good communicator). She makes no experiments with language, like Joyce; as Elizabeth Bowen wrote in her introduction to *Frost in May*, her style is 'as precise, clear and unweighty as Jane Austen's', and the work could be read with pleasure by a twelve-year-old girl.

The novel was turned down by one publisher's reader on the grounds that it was 'too slight to be of interest to anyone'.[123] Perhaps we are all too inclined to assume that a female child's experiences in an all-female community cannot be important. We know, too, that many people have written thinly-disguised autobiographical novels about being misunderstood and rejected, and that most of these novels are worthless. But even though almost all of Antonia White's fiction is based on her own life, that does not invalidate it as art. And most of us read it with fascination.

Nanda is a portrait of the artist as a young girl. But she is also Everyman, or every child who is suddenly thrust into a new and bewildering environment. We follow her into this world, which is strange to most of us, learn its rules with her and suffer with her when she breaks them. The first and most basic of these rules is that 'you've got to learn to do things you don't like' (1). This point is rammed home by the little stories which the nuns are constantly telling the children (the lost bride, the child with the pin through her ear, the saint whose brother snubs her). They are not to seek to please themselves because they are on earth solely in order to do the will of God; indeed the earth itself exists for no other reason:

The donkey in the paddock reminded her that all donkeys have crosses on their backs since the day Our Lord rode into Jerusalem; the robin's breast was red because one of his ancestors had splashed his feathers with the Precious Blood trying to peck away the crown of thorns. The clover and the shamrock were a symbol of the Blessed Trinity, the sunflower was a saint turning always towards God, the speedwell had been white till Our Lady's blue mantle brushed it as she walked in the fields of Nazareth. When Nanda heard a cock crow, it cried: '*Christus natus est*'; the cows lowed '*Ubi? Ubi?*' and the lambs down at the community farm bleated 'Be-e-thlehem'. (2)

Nanda is 'supersaturated' in dogma (the word is Joyce's), as, at the other end of the religious spectrum, was the young Edmund Gosse, whose classic *Father and Son* appeared the year before Antonia went to Roehampton. In it, he describes how, in the end, 'no compromise' with his father's religion was possible and how he 'took a human being's privilege to fashion his inner life for himself'.[124] It is Nanda's inner life, and the nuns' refusal to compromise, which are the real centre of *Frost in May*.

Nanda is 'one of those children who cannot help behaving well' (1). At no time does she have any doubts about her religion and she is anxious to please the authorities and pass her first test by winning the pink ribbon. But we are in a world of strange values. The good behaviour which would win her high praise in an ordinary school is mocked by Mother Frances because 'God doesn't care about namby-pamby goodness, you know' (2). She rebels, briefly, and breaks a rule in public. This could be seen as an example of the pressures which will finally drive her mad (in *Beyond the Glass*); it also makes a theological point.

The nuns are aware throughout that Nanda is in danger of spiritual pride, which is the ultimate sin in their eyes. She is prepared to keep all the rules and do whatever the Church wishes, provided she need not surrender her inner core of personality. Her greatest fear is that she may have to become a nun – in gratitude for her father's conversion, or Clare Rockingham's, or perhaps because that is the only way she can satisfy God. In the episode where she worries about her vow of perpetual virginity, the movements of the child's mind, as she puzzles over the mysterious ways of authority, are conveyed very well:

Was her promise binding? . . . . Even the thought of going back on a promise to God might be a mortal sin. It took three things, she knew, to make a mortal sin: grave matter, full knowledge, and full consent. The matter was grave enough, certainly. And though she was not quite clear what virginity actually was, she knew, that with the one exception of Our Lady, one could not be a virgin and married as well. Besides, St Joseph was always spoken of as Our Lady's spouse, so probably a spouse was not the same thing as a husband. As to full consent, she had been eight when she made the vow and seven is the age of reason. (4)

As a more sophisticated teenager, she protests 'I'm prepared to be as devout as you like, if I can only have a little time to myself . . . . It's impossible to think about God and Religion every minute of one's day . . . . I don't want poetry and pictures and things to be messages from God. I don't mind their being that as well, if you like, but not only that . . . . I want them to be complete in themselves' (9).

Antonia White became estranged from the Church partly because she feared that she would only be allowed to write orthodox books. From a very early age, she had been conscious of herself as a writer. Her characters are almost too consciously 'literary'; it is hard to believe that real children would walk about reciting poetry, sometimes in French. Nanda's developing conflict with her teachers is played out almost wholly in terms of books. First there is the confiscated copy of *Dream Days*; this reminds us of another important point, that the girls are not encouraged to have special friends. Then there is Francis Thompson's poetry which excites her as she has not been excited by her First Communion; 'this new feeling, whatever it was, had nothing to do with God' (5). Finally, there is her own early novel which causes her to be expelled and have a change of heart.

The nuns do not agree with Dorothy Sayers's thesis that Christians must strive to do their work as well as possible for the glory of God. They are quite prepared to spoil the school play rather than let one of the girls get too involved in her part. As the cynical Leonie says, 'there's nothing worse for the Catholic character than to do something it really enjoys' (9). Mortifying one's senses (as Nanda and Stephen both do in their respective novels) can be seen as a healthy spiritual exercise. The notes from her retreat say bluntly:

A saint said it was dangerous to walk through a beautiful wood . . . . Look for God in everything . . . . Even beauty often poisoned. Choose friends for solid piety, not for superficial good looks or accomplishments. Give up a friendship if it tends to hinder you in the practice of your religion. (7)

'I thought it meant giving up everything I cared for, renouncing all human pleasure, all love of human beings, all delight in natural things and in art and poetry unless they were directly "religious" and "edifying",'[125] Antonia White wrote after her reconversion. A crucial scene in *Frost in May* comes when Mother Radcliffe opens the letter in which Nanda compares Clare Rockingham's eyes to 'chips of emerald' (8). Her feelings of affection, and her developing skill as a writer, are both attacked. But, for the author, the 'chips of emerald' which signify art and spontaneous delight of all kinds are valuable and necessary in their own right, and she will not give them up.

The novel was written during her lapsed period. Yet it is clear to a careful reader that she does not, like Gosse and Joyce, reject the Church completely. Stephen Dedalus tears himself away from his religion and family, declaring that he will dedicate himself to being an artist and 'will not serve'. Nanda is expelled from the convent weeping and protesting; her childish novel abused; her worst grief the knowledge of having offended her terrifying father (who will become a more prominent character in the other three books). The nun who assures her, calmly and kindly, that 'all this is for your own good' (15), appears to speak with great authority.

The Lippington method of educating children is bound to shock us (and the snobbery which is mixed up with it makes it all the more hateful). Yet there is no denying the nuns' extraordinary, almost frightening dedication. Nanda's mother, who is very much the traditional woman, pities them:

> 'Those poor young women. Just think, they've given up *everything*' . . . . Then, with an understanding smile she turned to Nanda: 'Of course, there must be a kind of happiness in their lives. No responsibilities, you know'. (4)

But of course it is perfectly clear that she understands nothing. The reader will probably share Nanda's recoil when the light-hearted Hilary becomes a nun, but her friends tell her that she does not understand either:

> '. . . it does seem rather horrible, somehow. She was so gay and all that.'

'People who become nuns often are.'   (13)

The death of Mother Frances reminds us of several
bewildering things. There is the mystery of death itself, the
mystery of the hidden rooms where the nuns live, the mystery
of why Mother Frances suddenly becomes gentle and humble.
Afterwards, when we hear about her early life, we are confronted
with the question which comes up at intervals throughout the
novel – why normal young women with everything to make
them happy should choose to be nuns.

For Nanda, attracted by what Mary McCarthy called 'the
sense of mystery and wonder'[126] in Catholicism, yet repelled by
the demands it makes, becoming a nun is impossible. The only
thing she can be sure of is that God will make further demands
on her, and this duly happens in the last chapter. She is
turned out into an alien world and told that she must give up
her friends. But there is a consolation; Clare Rockingham will
be allowed to become a Catholic. This is an important point;
something very similar happens at the end of *Beyond the Glass*. It
is hinted that, in some incomprehensible way, God has accepted
Nanda's humiliation in exchange for Clare's conversion.

Nanda does not question Mother Radcliffe's clear statement
that her pain is necessary, and that the only thing which
matters is God's will. She cannot 'break away without a sense
of mutilation' (7), and when she has the chance of leaving
Lippington she does not take it – this in spite of all her
rebellious and non-heroic impulses, which the reader will well
understand. The book, then, is not quite the devastating
indictment of a Catholic education which it appears to be.
Joyce, so much more 'difficult' a writer than Antonia White,
ends his book on a much less ambiguous note.

In later life Antonia White wrote that *Frost in May* was

> sincere as far as it goes, but it is superficial. Perhaps it could
> not be otherwise for to give a true picture of a convent school
> one would have to have some understanding of the spiritual
> life of the nuns themselves and its relation to their teaching
> activities. With a child's egotism I had no notion that nuns
> might have conflicts and difficulties of their own.[127]

This is surely too harsh. The nuns have ample opportunity to

state their views in the course of the book, and as for their
hidden lives – the whole point is that these are almost impossible
for outsiders to understand. Her later novels were to prove that
she worked much better when she concentrated on the
experience of a central figure.

It is helpful to know that these three novels – *The Lost
Traveller*, *The Sugar House* and *Beyond the Glass* – were written one
after another, more than fifteen years later than *Frost in May*,
and after she had returned to the Church and absorbed the
teachings of Freud. Nanda has been renamed Clara, but she
and her parents are obviously the same people. Many of the
events of her life as a young adult appear in these books.

Antonia wanted *The Lost Traveller* to be 'something more
ambitious . . . a "proper" novel, not seen only through the eyes
of one person as it is in *Frost in May*, but through the eyes of her
father, her mother and even those old great aunts in the
country.'[128] Here the Antonia-figure has left the convent and
instead of living in an ordered world where everything is
decided for her, is in a secular society which is largely indifferent
to her values. The title suggests that she is liable quickly to lose
her way. So does the motto, from St Augustine, 'every heart is
closed to every other heart'. Clara's sense of dislocation is
conveyed in the scene where she tries to pray but soon becomes
aware of 'the discomfort of the hard wood against her silk-clad
knees':

> At one moment one was on one's knees imploring the grace
> to submit wholly to the will of God, however painful: the
> next one was in a rage because a hem line dropped a quarter
> of an inch. How did all these things fit together?   (7,3)

The Clara of these novels is a lukewarm Catholic, practising
her religion out of habit but preoccupied with choosing a
husband and finding a firm identity for herself. But it is clear
that the religion she learned at Lippington is not going to leave
her alone. We are frequently reminded of the old Irishwoman's
remark on the first page of *Frost in May*: 'To think of the three
of us in the omnibus in a Protestant country and everyone of us
Catholics.' The war, which is going on throughout the action of
The Lost Traveller, has very little importance. But the Church is
inescapable; when Isabel falls in love, the man turns out to be a

lapsed Catholic; all the women in Clara's touring company are Catholics; when she takes a house in Chelsea with her husband there just happens to be a Catholic church – 'stern, heavy, uncompromising' (*The Sugar House*, 2,11) – on the other side of the road.

The Lost Traveller is the weakest of the quartet. The central incident – the death of little Charles – was, apparently, invented, and perhaps this was why the author was unable to make it really moving. Its only significance seems to be that it increases Clara's sense of guilt. And although her parents are vivid characters and become more vivid in the later novels, it passes belief that each of them would have a first-time passionate encounter with someone else on the day they learn about their daughter's crisis. But this long and rather scrappy book does establish that Isabel, who merely wants her child to be happy, is wiser than Claude with his rigid views of how a young Catholic girl should behave. It also shows that Clara is drifting, and perhaps disintegrating. She is 'so used to obeying other people that it was almost impossible to obey herself' (4,3).

The world, as the nuns acknowledge (4,6), is 'a difficult place for a Catholic girl'. Since the war, the atmosphere has changed and fewer and fewer people profess religion. Clara sometimes goes back to the convent, to the family acres in Sussex and to the Catholic household of Maryhall, which give her some idea of what an ordered life might be. But neither the nuns, the old aunts, nor the saintly Lady Cressett – a traditional Catholic woman whose life is one of sacrifice – really understand her problem. Lady Cressett says openly that she is 'old-fashioned' and thinks that all women should marry young or go into convents. But Clara realises that to live like this requires qualities which she 'did not even begin to possess' (*The Sugar House*, 1,11).

The Clara of *The Sugar House* finds that she can easily support herself in post-war Britain, but organising her inner life is far more difficult. Like Flora Mayor and Dorothy Sayers, Antonia White had tried being an actress and an advertising copywriter. Her feelings seem to have been much the same as theirs; these experiences offered freedom of a sort, and money, but in the long run they were profoundly unsatisfying. Clara's life as an actress is 'slipshod' and bears no relation to what she really wants; the advertisements which bring in easy money leave her with plenty of time on her hands, which she does not know how to fill. She believes herself to be nothing but a 'mediocre actress with the knack of writing advertisements and cheap short stories' (1,8), and the unpleasant Stephen, who speaks for many other people, assures her that women cannot write serious novels.

Clara does, in fact, have enough talent to write one good short story. But she has enormous difficulties about doing this, because her father denounced her childish novel. The influence of Freud – who is mentioned, apparently casually, in the sixth chapter – is felt throughout. In himself, Claude is a decent man who is obviously devoted to Clara, yet his influence on her has been wholly negative. She is guilty about mixing with people, like actors and artists, whom he would disapprove of; frightened that he will walk into the Sugar House and denounce her sloppy way of life. She has a rare moment of open rebellion – 'Why shouldn't I live as I want to?' (2,7) – but her guilt and fear are not to be shaken off. It is not surprising that she marries a man who is as different as possible from her father. But Archie has not grown up either and there is a false sweetness about the 'sugar house' where they live and their 'nice games of trains'. As the house disintegrates around them (its sole advantage being that it is not her parents' home), she realises that abstinence is destroying her, and that her 'numbed body' cannot produce a child 'any more than her numbed mind could produce even a fragment of living work' (2,11). Clara's madness in the next book is clearly foreshadowed in this one, particularly in the late chapters about her life in the Sugar House. While the first half is not particularly impressive, the second becomes steadily more powerful, with haunting poetic undertones. She feels that 'I'm not *any* person' (2,8); that she has no true identity but is like the chameleon which changes colour according to where it is. At other times she believes that she is 'inwardly corrupt' and a 'monster' (2,8). Freudian ideas about the unconscious mind and repressed sexuality reappear when the boyish Archie builds a dam and she has to 'use all her self-control not to pull away some of the stones and release the imprisoned water' (2,4).

Although she herself does nothing of value in Chelsea, its real significance for her is that it is 'a place where people worked'. It makes her pray not to be 'a messy amateur' (2,4). Her

encounter with Gundry, after months of drifting, is crucial, and
not just because he reveals to her that she has a way out. Even
the fact that he shows her what has been lacking in her
marriage is less important than his description of what his
painting means to him. Like her, he has produced 'muck',
which sells far better than serious work. But he is now dedicated
to the kind of art which really satisfies his nature, and Clara
feels that this dedication is a kind of religion, perhaps more
meaningful than the form she has been taught. The ordinary
things in his studio suddenly take on an extraordinary beauty:

> Some crumpled brown paper, torn and showing patches of
> the white canvas it covered, became a pile of rocks with rifts
> of snow; a naked mirror propped against the wall, reflecting
> tubes and brushes at an odd angle, became an aquarium
> with silver fish and spiky plants glimmering through dusky
> water.   (2,13)

It is 'like coming to life'. Only a glimpse of what this new life
might be is offered, and the book ends with her leaving Archie,
realising that she has treated him selfishly, and terrified of the
'unknown' ordeal which lies ahead. Yet it is clear that only by
submitting to that ordeal can she break out of a sterile and
meaningless way of life.

But worse ordeals are to come. In the sequel, *Beyond the Glass*,
Clara comes out of her apathetic drifting state into one of
heightened awareness, too intense to be compatible with normal
life, in which she constantly slides over the borders of sanity.
This is Antonia White's greatest novel, better than Sylvia
Plath's more famous *Bell Jar* which has the same subject, and –
in spite of popular opinion – even better than *Frost in May*. All
her best work is concerned with overwhelming experiences –
immersion in a Catholic school, or, as in this case, love and
madness.

The novel begins quietly, with funny and convincing pictures
of her parents and of Clive Heron. There is almost no hint, at
first, that Clara will go mad. The only obvious thing about her
is that up to this point she has allowed others to manage her
life, taking no responsibility for the ending of her marriage
which she cannot be said to have really chosen. She is afraid of
sex, unenthusiastic about her religion (but prepared to keep its

rules), and still, at the age of twenty-two, childishly afraid of her father and in need of his support. For perceptive readers, she demonstrates some of the early signs of schizophrenia:

> it was not she who was stripping hangers and throwing armfuls of clothes into suitcases but some callous, efficient stranger. She herself was lying on the unmade bed, staring blankly at the cracks in the sugar-pink ceiling. (1,3)

In her madness, Clara breaks into two people; one performing actions which have no connection with her conscious will while another part of her mind is busy recording what is happening. But her madness comes on slowly. In the early chapters her mental state is conveyed by the image of a pane of glass with Clara on one side, unable to communicate with the people beyond it. She is upset at the thought of having to look at Archie through a glass door, 'glaring at him speechlessly like a fish in an aquarium' (2,1). This foreshadows the mad scene where she knows she is in the same room as Richard but cannot hear or speak to him. 'He was close to her now but she could not get through to him nor he to her' (3,9). She has the same kind of experience when she imagines she is a salmon suffocating just out of reach of 'the life-giving waterfall' (4,1). Water is another central image in *Beyond the Glass*, usually the dark water of the Thames which the author identifies with 'a continuous stream of life' (2,2).

It has been said that this is a novel about love. Clara's feelings for Richard are sometimes described in hackneyed woman's-magazine terms – 'she forgot everything but that they had found each other' (3,2) – and the references to *Romeo and Juliet* are not strictly necessary. But we have no difficulty believing in the essential truth of their relationship – sudden, complete, and overwhelming. The strange fact that they can communicate telepathically (which has nothing to do with the Church's version of the supernatural) makes their romance even more intense and enchanted. Yet we are hardly surprised, after Clara comes back to normality, to find that Richard is no longer there. We have already sensed that he is a fairly prosaic young man, that there is something tragic about their love, and that Clara is not destined to be happy in the ordinary way.

Such happiness as there is seems to come from observing the

rituals and obeying the laws of the Catholic church. Isabel sometimes rages against these laws, particularly the bans on divorce and contraception, and there is no doubt that the author had a lot of sympathy with her. Nevertheless, Clara is only able to bring order and meaning into her life when she seriously tries to practise her religion. Archie calls it 'rather as if you were in the hell of a panic on the way to an operation and knew somehow you'd just manage not to get off the trolley' (1,3). It should be stressed that the author is not trying to convert anyone. Catholicism is simply shown to be part of Clara's nature, and also part of her problem. Other people, the majority who can do without it, are surprised by the way Catholics 'let it interfere with their ordinary lives' (3,2). One element, as Clara has already learned at her convent school, is the sacrifice of individual wishes. So, when she is praying seriously, she prays not to marry Richard but for 'grace to accept whatever Your will is for both of us' (3,4). At another point, realising the shallowness of her 'refusal to experience' the war, she asks to be put to the test and given some share in the suffering it caused.

This, of course, is about to happen. When Clara recovers, she finds that Richard is married; the fact that he has become a Catholic is just one more barrier between them. Yet, as at the end of *Frost in May*, she knows that she ought to be glad. Her own suffering has, perhaps, paved the way for him. The rosary he leaves her is like a 'detaining hand' which holds her back from suicide (4,9).

Strangely enough the first time that Clara tries to walk into the river is just after she has been trying to defend the dogma of the Immaculate Conception. (Almost the same thing happens in a short story based on her madness, 'The House of Clouds'.[129]) Antonia White had suggested elsewhere that religion should be approached not through the reason but through intuition. 'Don't try and come it over me with those official proofs. Any logician could dispose of them in five minutes' (2,3), Clive warns Clara. Indeed Clara's problem may be that she is trying too hard to behave beautifully, to be a good daughter to her father and to the Church, to keep all the rules. Two of the doctors who treat her state that she is suffering from what we have learned to call repression: 'Controls have a way of breaking down, you know' (3,8) and, after she has ripped up a fur coat

with her bare hands: 'It's remarkable what people *can* do when
the brakes are off' (4,8). In Freudian terms, Clara's madness
can be seen as a struggle between the three aspects of her
personality. For long stretches of time the id takes over, when
she hits, fights, and spits out food. She identifies with animals
during this time and is vaguely conscious that the nurses think
she is not quite human, 'one of them' (4,1). 'They' are the mad
women who live in a horrifying world, just hinted at by the
slogan

Baby
Blood
Murder

on the wall of the yard. Gradually her ego regroups its forces
and she becomes more rational, conscious that she can only get
out of the asylum by making a determined effort to distance
herself from the mad women. The superego, too, is present in
flashes, as when she decides not to inform on the bullying
nurse. At other points in her illness she turns to religion to save
her. In the last scene, her superego is dominant and she is
recognisably the same person as the child in *Frost in May* who
'cannot help behaving well'. She accepts that she has lost
Richard, does not complain and feels no resentment against
Kathleen. Where she does not behave as her father wants is by
refusing to deny the experience of having been mad. It was
real; it had some sort of meaning; one day she may be able to
'piece it together' (4,8). She will accept certain voluntary
restrictions, but she will not lose touch with the dark
unacknowledged forces which have been revealed to her.

The world of madness and poetry which Antonia White
created in *Beyond the Glass* cannot be forgotten, once experienced.
If she had written more novels like this and *Frost in May*, she
would certainly have achieved a higher reputation in her
lifetime. But, as we know, there was no sequel. Clara in the
year 1922, sane but on her own and with no idea of what is to
happen next, is a profoundly modern heroine. It was a wise
instinct that made the author leave her there.

Notes

1. Ruth First and Ann Scott, *Olive Schreiner* (London, Deutsch, 1980), p. 23.
2. Dan Jacobson, Introduction to *The Story of an African Farm* (Harmondsworth, Penguin, 1971 edn).
3. First and Scott, *Olive Schreiner*, p. 46.
4. Quoted by S. C. Cronwright-Schreiner, *The Life of Olive Schreiner* (London, T. Fisher Unwin, 1924), p. 222.
5. Quoted by First and Scott, *Olive Schreiner*, p. 121.
6. S. C. Cronwright-Schreiner (ed.), *The Letters of Olive Schriner 1876–1920* (London, T. Fisher Unwin, 1924), pp. 182–3.
7. Cronwright-Schreiner, *Life*, p. vii.
8. Ibid, p. 161.
9. Ibid, p. 316.
10. First and Scott, *Olive Schreiner*, p. 258.
11. Ibid, p. 326.
12. Ibid, p. 157.
13. Cronwright-Schreiner, *Letters*, p. 321.
14. S. C. Cronwright-Schreiner, Introduction to *From Man to Man*.
15. Virginia Woolf, *Three Guineas* (London, Hogarth Press, 1938), Ch. 2.
16. Cronwright-Schreiner, *Letters*, p. 343.
17. Percy Lubbock, *Portrait of Edith Wharton* (London, Cape, 1947), Ch. 14.
18. Edith Wharton, *A Backward Glance* (New York, Appleton, 1933), Ch. 1.
19. Ibid.
20. Ibid, Ch. 3.
21. R. W. B. Lewis, *Edith Wharton, A Biography* (London, Constable, 1975), p. 66.
22. *A Backward Glance*, Ch. 6.
23. Ibid.
24. Ibid, Ch. 7.
25. Lubbock, *Portrait*, Ch. 5.
26. Lewis, *Edith Wharton*, p. 347.
27. Ibid, p. 220.
28. Ibid, p. 317–18.
29. Lubbock, *Portrait*, Ch. 10.
30. Lewis, *Edith Wharton*, p. 180.
31. Preface to *The Ghost Stories of Edith Wharton* (London, Constable, 1975).
32. Lewis, *Edith Wharton*, p. 452.

33. Ibid, p. 131.

34. Cronwright-Schreiner, *Letters*, p. 319.

35. *A Backward Glance*, Ch. 9.

36. Lewis, *Edith Wharton*, p. 326.

37. 'The Other Two', first published in 1904, is reprinted in *Roman Fever* (New York, Scribner, 1964).

38. *A Backward Glance*, Ch. 8.

39. Ibid, Ch. 7.

40. In *Old New York* (New York, Appleton, 1924).

41. Lewis, *Edith Wharton*, p. xiii.

42. Sybil Oldfield, *Spinsters of this Parish: The Life and Times of F. M. Mayor and Mary Sheepshanks* (London, Virago, 1984), p. 243.

43. Ibid, p. 39.

44. Ibid, p. 41.

45. Ibid, p. 75.

46. Ibid, p. 276.

47. Ibid, p. 136.

48. F. M. Mayor, *The Rector's Daughter* (London, Hogarth Press, 1924), Ch. 27.

49. Oldfield, *Spinsters*, p. 201.

50. Ibid, p. 203.

51. Ibid, p. 166.

52. Ibid, p. 172.

53. Ibid, p. 315.

54. Margaret Oliphant, *Kirsteen* (London, Macmillan, 1890), reprinted as an Everyman Classic, 1984.

55. Oldfield, *Spinsters*, p. 152.

56. Ibid, p. 174.

57. Ibid, p. 241.

58. Katherine Mansfield, 'To Stanislaw Wyspianski', in Allen Curnow (ed.), *The Penguin Book of New Zealand Verse* (Auckland, Blackwood and Janet Paul, 1966).

59. John Middleton Murry (ed.), *The Letters of Katherine Mansfield* (London, Constable, 1928), vol. 2, p. 199.

60. Curnow, *New Zealand Verse*, p. 27.

61. Ruth Elvish Mantz and J. Middleton Murry, *The Life of Katherine Mansfield* (London, Constable, 1933), p. 208.

62. Ibid, p. 224.

63. Antony Alpers, *The Life of Katherine Mansfield* (London, Cape, 1980), p. 55.

64. Vincent O'Sullivan and Margaret Scott (eds), *The Collected Letters of Katherine Mansfield, Volume One, 1903–1917* (Oxford, Clarendon Press, 1984), p. 42.

65. Mantz and Murry, *Life*, p. 279.

66. Ibid, p. 270.

67. Ibid, p. 239.

68. John Middleton Murry, *Katherine Mansfield and other Literary Studies* (London 1959), p. 91.

69. John Middleton Murry (ed.), *Letters of Katherine Mansfield to John Middleton Murry* (London, Constable, 1951), pp. 578–9.

70. Middleton Murry, *Letters*, (1928), vol. 2, p. 160.

71. Mantz and Murry, *Life*, pp. 14–15.

72. O'Sullivan and Scott, *Collected Letters*, p. 261.

73. *Letters to John Middleton Murry*, pp. 419–20.

74. Ibid, p. 566.

75. Introductory Note to Katherine Mansfield, *The Dove's Nest* (London, Constable, 1923).

76. Middleton Murry, *Letters*, (1928), vol. 2, p. 268.

77. Anne Olivier Bell (ed.), *The Diary of Virginia Woolf, Volume 2, 1920–24* (Harmondsworth, Penguin, 1978), p. 227.

78. F. R. Leavis, *D. H. Lawrence, Novelist* (London, Chatto & Windus, 1955), p. 295.

79. Mantz and Murry, *Life*, p. 7.

80. Ibid, p. 92.

81. *Letters to John Middleton Murry*, p. 149.

82. O'Sullivan and Scott, *Collected Letters*, p. 331.

83. Alpers, *Katherine Mansfield*, p. 283.

84. *Letters to John Middleton Murry*, p. 380.

85. Ibid, p. 392.

86. Middleton Murry, *Letters* (1928), vol. 2, p. 152.

87. Mantz and Murry, *Life*, p. 2.

88. Alpers, *Katherine Mansfield*, p. 341.

89. Middleton Murry, *Letters* (1928), vol. 2, p. 134.

90. Ibid, vol. 2, p. 120.

91. O'Sullivan and Scott, *Collected Letters*, p. 124.

92. James Brabazon, *Dorothy L. Sayers* (London, Gollancz, 1981), pp. 262–3.

93. Dorothy L. Sayers, 'Gaudy Night', in Denys Kilham Roberts (ed.), *Titles to Fame* (London, Nelson, 1937), pp. 76, 88.

94. Dorothy L. Sayers, 'Are Women Human?', in *Unpopular Opinions* (London, Gollancz, 1946), p. 115.

95. Brabazon, *Dorothy L. Sayers*, p. 95.

96. Q. D. Leavis, 'The Case of Miss Dorothy Sayers', *Scrutiny*, December 1937.

97. Roberts, *Titles to Fame*, p. 77.

98. Ibid, p. 78.

99. Brabazon, *Dorothy L. Sayers*, p. 253.

100. Agatha Christie, *Appointment with Death* (London, Collins, 1938), Ch. 6.

101. Q. D. Leavis, cited n. 96 above.

102. Dorothy L. Sayers, 'The Human-Not-Quite-Human', in *Unpopular Opinions*, p. 120.

103. Roberts, *Titles to Fame*, p. 81.

104. Ibid, p. 79.

105. *Unpopular Opinions*, p. 106.

106. Ibid, p. 107.

107. Ibid, p. 113.

108. Sheila Jeffreys, *The Spinster and her Enemies: Feminism and Sexuality 1880–1930* (London, Pandora Press, 1985), p. 191.

109. *Unpopular Opinions*, p. 121.

110. Antonia White, *The Hound and the Falcon* (London, Longman, 1965), Virago 1980 edn, p. 82.

111. Mary McCarthy, *Memories of a Catholic Girlhood* (London, Heinemann, 1957), p. 76.

112. Antonia White, 'A Child of the Five Wounds', in Susan Chitty (ed.), *As Once in May* (London, Virago, 1983), p. 162.

113. *The Hound and the Falcon*, p. 24.

114. Tom Hopkinson, *Of This Our Time* (London, Hutchinson, 1982), p. 140.

115. *The Hound and the Falcon*, p. 159.

116. Ibid, p. 7.

117. Ibid, p. 152.

118. Ibid, p. 5.

119. Ibid, p. 104.

120. Susan Chitty, *Now to my Mother* (London, Weidenfeld & Nicolson, 1985), p. 158.

121. Susan Chitty, Introduction to *As Once in May*, p. 7.

122. *The Hound and the Falcon*, p. 115.

123. Quoted by Carmen Callil, Introduction to Virago editions of *The Lost Traveller*, *The Sugar House* and *Beyond the Glass* (London, 1979).

124. Edmund Gosse, *Father and Son* (London, Heinemann, 1907), Epilogue.

125. *The Hound and the Falcon*, p. 49.

126. McCarthy, *Memories*, p. xxxiv.

127. *The Hound and the Falcon*, p. 154.

128. Quoted by Carmen Callil, Introduction to *The Lost Traveller* (London 1979).

129. In *Strangers* (London, Harvill Press, 1954).

Bibliography

PRIMARY SOURCES

Mansfield, Katherine
    Collected Stories (London, Constable, 1945)
Mayor, F. M.
    The Third Miss Symons (London, Sidgwick and Jackson, 1913)
    The Rector's Daughter (London, Hogarth Press, 1924).
Sayers, Dorothy L.
    Whose Body? (London, T. Fisher Unwin, 1923)
    Clouds of Witness (London, T. Fisher Unwin, 1926)
    Unnatural Death (London, Ernest Benn, 1927)
    The Unpleasantness at the Bellona Club (London, Ernest Benn, 1928)
    Lord Peter Views the Body (London, Gollancz, 1928)
    (with Robert Eustace) *The Documents in the Case* (London, Ernest Benn, 1930)
    Strong Poison (London, Gollancz, 1930)
    Five Red Herrings (London, Gollancz, 1931)
    Have his Carcase (London, Gollancz, 1932)
    Murder Must Advertise (London, Gollancz, 1933)
    Hangman's Holiday (London, Gollancz, 1933)
    The Nine Tailors (London, Gollancz, 1934)
    Gaudy Night (London, Gollancz, 1935)
    Busman's Honeymoon (London, Gollancz, 1937)
Schreiner, Olive
    The Story of an African Farm (London, Chapman & Hall, 1883)
    Dreams (London, Ernest Benn, 1890)
    Trooper Peter Halket of Mashonaland (Leipzig, Tauchnitz, 1897).
    From Man to Man (New York and London, Harper, 1927)
Wharton, Edith
    The House of Mirth (New York, Scribner, 1905)
    The Fruit of the Tree (New York, Scribner, 1907)
    Ethan Frome (New York, Scribner, 1911)
    The Reef (New York, Appleton, 1912)
    The Custom of the Country (New York, Scribner, 1913)
    Summer (New York, Scribner, 1917)
    The Age of Innocence (New York, Tyler, 1920)
    The Children (New York, Appleton, 1928)

Madame de Treymes (stories) (New York, Scribner, 1970)
Roman Fever (stories) (New York, Scribner, 1964)
White, Antonia
Frost in May (London, Desmond Harmsworth, 1933)
The Lost Traveller (London, Eyre & Spottiswoode, 1950)
The Sugar House (London, Eyre & Spottiswoode, 1952)
Beyond the Glass (London, Eyre & Spottiswoode, 1954)
Strangers (stories) (London, Harvill Press, 1954).

SECONDARY SOURCES

Alphers, Antony, *The Life of Katherine Mansfield* (London, Cape, 1980)
Baker, Ida, *Katherine Mansfield: The Memories of L. M.* (London, Michael Joseph, 1971)
Bell, Millicent, *Edith Wharton and Henry James* (London, Peter Owen, 1965)
Berkman, Sylvia, *Katherine Mansfield, A Critical Study* (New Haven, Yale University Press, 1951)
Brabazon, James, *Dorothy L. Sayers* (London, Gollancz, 1981)
Buchanan-Gould, Vera, *Not Without Honour, The Life and Writings of Olive Schreiner* (London, Hutchinson, 1948)
Chitty, Susan, *Now to my Mother, A very personal memoir of Antonia White* (London, Weidenfeld & Nicolson, 1985)
—— (ed.), *As Once in May, The Early Autobiography of Antonia White and other writings* (London, Virago 1983)
Cronwright-Schreiner, S. C., *The Life of Olive Schreiner* (London, T. Fisher Unwin, 1924)
—— (ed.), *The Letters of Olive Schreiner 1876–1920* (London, T. Fisher Unwin, 1924)
First, Ruth and Scott, Ann, *Olive Schreiner* (London, Deutsch, 1980)
Hankin, C. A., *Katherine Mansfield and her Confessional Stories* (London, Macmillan, 1983)
Hopkinson, Tom, *Of This Our Time* (London, Hutchinson, 1982)
Howe, Irving (ed.), *Edith Wharton, A Collection of Critical Essays* (New Jersey, Prentice-Hall, 1962)
Jeffreys, Sheila, *The Spinster and her Enemies: Feminism and Sexuality 1880–1930* (London, Pandora Press, 1985)
Lea, F. A., *The Life of John Middleton Murry* (London, Methuen, 1959)
Leavis, Q. D., 'The Case of Miss Dorothy Sayers', *Scrutiny*, December 1937
Lewis, R. W. B., *Edith Wharton, A Biography* (London, Constable, 1975)
Lindberg, Gary B., *Edith Wharton and the Novel of Manners* (Charlottesville, University Press of Virginia, 1975)
Lubbock, Percy, *Portrait of Edith Wharton* (London, Cape, 1947)
Magalaner, Marvin, *The Fiction of Katherine Mansfield* (Carbondale and Edwardsville, Southern Illinois University Press, 1971)
Mantz, Ruth Elvish and Murry, J. M., *The Life of Katherine Mansfield* (London, Constable, 1933)
Meyers, Jeffrey, *Katherine Mansfield, A Biography* (London, Hamish Hamilton, 1978)
Murry, John Middleton, *Between Two Worlds* (London, Cape, 1935)

—— (ed.), *Journal of Katherine Mansfield* (London, Constable, 1927)

—— (ed.), *The Letters of Katherine Mansfield* (London, Constable, 1928)

—— (ed.), *Novels and Novelists,* by Katherine Mansfield (London, Constable, 1930)

—— (ed.), *Letters of Katherine Mansfield to John Middleton Murry, 1913–1922* (London, Constable, 1951)

Nevius, Blake, *Edith Wharton* (Berkeley, University of California Press, 1953)

Oldfield, Sybil, *Spinsters of this Parish: The Life and Times of F. M. Mayor and Mary Sheepshanks* (London, Virago, 1984)

Roberts, Denys Kilham (ed.), *Titles to Fame* (London, Nelson, 1937)

Sayers, Dorothy L., *Unpopular Opinions* (London, Gollancz, 1946)

Schreiner, Olive, *Woman and Labour* (London, T. Fisher Unwin, 1911)

Sinclair, May, *Life and Death of Harriett Frean* (London, Collins, 1922)

Walton, Geoffrey, *Edith Wharton* (New Jersey, Fairleigh Dickinson University Press, 1970)

Wharton, Edith, *The Writing of Fiction* (New York, Scribner, 1925)

——, *A Backward Glance* (New York, Appleton, 1933)

White, Antonia, *The Hound and the Falcon* (London, Longman, 1965)

Wolff, Cynthia Griffin, *A Feast of Words, The Triumph of Edith Wharton* (New York, Oxford University Press, 1977)

Index